CAMBRIDGE PRIMARY
Mathematics

Learner's Book

5

Emma Low

CAMBRIDGE
UNIVERSITY PRESS

CAMBRIDGE
UNIVERSITY PRESS

University Printing House, Cambridge CB2 8BS, United Kingdom

Cambridge University Press is part of the University of Cambridge.

It furthers the University's mission by disseminating knowledge in the pursuit of education, learning and research at the highest international levels of excellence.

Information on this title: education.cambridge.org

First published 2014
8th printing 2016

Printed in the United Kingdom by Latimer Trend

A catalogue record for this publication is available from the British Library

ISBN 978-1-107-63822-8 Paperback

Cambridge University Press has no responsibility for the persistence or accuracy of URLs for external or third-party internet websites referred to in this publication, and does not guarantee that any content on such websites is, or will remain, accurate or appropriate.

....

Introduction

This *Learner's Book* is a supplementary resource that consolidates and reinforces mathematical learning alongside the *Cambridge Primary Mathematics Teacher's Resource 5* (9781107694361). It provides introductory investigations (Let's investigate) to encourage the application of mathematical knowledge, and numerous questions and activities to develop problem-solving skills.

Ideally, a session should be taught using the appropriate *Core activity* in the *Teacher's Resource 5*. The associated content in the *Learner's Book 5* can then be used for formative assessment at the end of a session, for homework or used for support in learning new vocabulary. There is generally a double page corresponding to each *Core activity* in the *Teacher's Resource 5* printed book. The *Core activity* that the page relates to is indicated at the bottom of the page.

Hints and tips are provided throughout to support the learners. They will appear as follows:

Write a list of number pairs to help you

Please note that the Learner's Book on its own does **not** cover all of the Cambridge Primary mathematics curriculum framework for Stage 5. You need to use it in conjunction with the Teacher's Resource 5 to ensure full coverage.

This publication is part of the *Cambridge Primary Maths* project. *Cambridge Primary Maths* is an innovative combination of curriculum and resources designed to support teachers and learners to succeed in primary mathematics through best-practice international maths teaching and a problem-solving approach.

Cambridge Primary Maths brings together the world-class Cambridge Primary mathematics curriculum from Cambridge International Examinations, high-quality publishing from Cambridge University Press and expertise in engaging online enrichment materials for the mathematics curriculum from NRICH.

Teachers have access to an online tool that maps resources and links to materials offered through the primary mathematics curriculum, NRICH and Cambridge Primary mathematics textbooks and e-books. These resources include engaging online activities, best-practice guidance and examples of *Cambridge Primary Maths* in action.

The Cambridge curriculum is dedicated to helping schools develop learners who are confident, responsible, reflective, innovative and engaged. It is designed to give learners the skills to problem solve effectively, apply mathematical knowledge and develop a holistic understanding of the subject.

The *Cambridge Primary Maths* textbooks provide best-in-class support for this problem-solving approach, based on pedagogical practice found in successful schools across the world. The engaging NRICH online resources help develop mathematical thinking and problem-solving skills. To get involved visit www.cie.org.uk/cambridgeprimarymaths

The benefits of being part of *Cambridge Primary Maths* are:
- the opportunity to explore a maths curriculum founded on the values of the University of Cambridge and best practice in schools
- access to an innovative package of online and print resources that can help bring the Cambridge Primary mathematics curriculum to life in the classroom.

This series is arranged to ensure that the curriculum is covered whilst
allowing teachers to use a flexible approach. The Scheme of Work for Stage 5
has been followed, though not in the same order and there will be some deviations. The components are:
- Teacher's Resource 5
  ISBN: 9781107694361 (printed book and CD-ROM).
- Learner's Book 5
  ISBN: 97811076638228 (printed book)
- Games Book 5
  ISBN: 9781107667815 (printed book and CD-ROM).

For associated NRICH activities, please visit the *Cambridge Primary Maths* project at www.cie.org.uk/cambridgeprimarymaths

Number

Place value

Vocabulary

ten thousand: is 10 times larger than one thousand $(10 \times 1000 = 10\,000)$.

hundred thousand: is 100 times larger than one thousand $(100 \times 1000 = 100\,000)$.

$\times 100$

Hth	Tth	Th	H	T	U
1	0	0	0	0	0

Let's investigate

Here are five digit cards.

Use three of these cards to make the missing number on the number line.

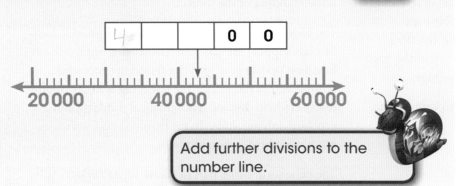

Add further divisions to the number line.

1 Look at this number: 950 302

(a) What does the digit 9 represent? (b) What does the digit 5 represent?

2 Write these numbers in figures.

(a) three hundred and thirty-five thousand, two hundred and seventy-one

(b) one hundred and five thousand and fifty

(c) one hundred and twenty thousand, two hundred and two

3 Write these numbers in words.

(a) 307 201 (b) 577 006 (c) 790 320

4 What number needs to be added or subtracted to change:

(a) 36 473 to 86 473 in one step?

(b) 206 070 to 204 070 in one step?

(c) 47 098 to 54 098 in one step?

Use a calculator to check your answers.

5 When you partition these numbers, what needs to go in each box? Discuss your answer with a partner.

(a) $806\,417 = \boxed{?} + 6000 + \boxed{?} + \boxed{?} + 7$

(b) $689\,567 = 600\,000 + \boxed{?} + \boxed{?} + 500 + \boxed{?} + \boxed{?}$

(c) $508\,208 = \boxed{?} + \boxed{?} + \boxed{?} + \boxed{?}$

6 What number needs to go in each box? Explain why.

$703\,842 = \boxed{?} + 3000 + \boxed{?} + \boxed{?} + 2$

7 Use the clues to solve this crossword.
Ask your teacher for a print out of it.
Write your answers in words.

Across
2. The digit in the units place in the number 742 793.
5. Seven groups of ten.
6. The digit in the ten thousands place in the number 842 793.

Down
1. The name for 0, 1, 2, 3, 4, 5, 6, 7, 8 and 9.
3. The digit in the hundred thousands place in the number 814 682.
4. This digit is used to hold an empty place in a number.

8 What number is equivalent to 130 thousand + 3 tens?

9 Work out the answers to these questions using mental methods:

(a) $358 \times 100 = \boxed{?}$ (b) $3000 \div 100 = \boxed{?}$ (c) $29 \times \boxed{?} = 2900$

(d) $2700 \div \boxed{?} = 27$ (e) $\boxed{?} \div 100 = 3040$

10 What is ten thousand subtract 1?

11 Which of these five numbers is 100 times larger than five hundred and fifty-five?

55.5 555 5550 $55\,500$ $555\,000$

Ordering and rounding

Let's investigate

Here are five numbers:

5505   5455   5045   5500   5050

Match each number to the correct letter A, B, C, D or E in the following table.

	Number rounded to the:		
	nearest 10	nearest 100	nearest 1000
A	5500	5500	6000
B	5050	5100	5000
C	5050	5000	5000
D	5460	5500	5000
E	5510	5500	6000

> You may find it easier to take the five starting numbers and round them to the nearest 10, 100 and 1000.

1 Look at the number line.
   2505 is 3000 when rounded to the nearest thousand.
   Round these numbers to the nearest thousand:
   (a) 3509   (b) 3499   (c) 4655

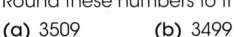

2 Look at the number line.
   2505 is 2500 when rounded to the nearest hundred.
   Round these numbers to the nearest hundred:
   (a) 3509   (b) 3499   (c) 4655

3 Look at the number line.
   2505 is 2510 when rounded to the nearest ten.
   Round these numbers to the nearest ten:
   (a) 3509   (b) 3499   (c) 4655

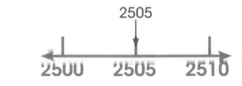

4 The highest point in the world is Mount Everest in Nepal.
   It is 8848 metres above sea level.
   Round 8848 to the nearest hundred metres.

5 5206 people dressed up as their favourite
story character to raise money for a hospital in London.

(a) Round 5206 to the nearest hundred.

(b) Round 5206 to the nearest ten.

6 Place these numbers in order of size, starting with the smallest.

(a) 6505   6550   5650   6555   5656

(b) 1234   2134   2413   1432   2341

7 Use the signs < or > to complete these statements.

(a) 3606 **?** 3660   (b) 7852 **?** 7825   (c) 5505 **?** 5050

8 Look at this table showing information about five mathematicians.

Name	Dates	Notes
Leonhard Euler	1707–1783	Introduced mathematical notation.
Carl Gauss	1777–1855	Famous for his mental ability.
Ada Lovelace	1815–1852	Often called the world's first computer programmer.
Isaac Newton	1642–1727	Worked on laws of motion.
Alan Turing	1912–1954	Created methods of code breaking.

Place the mathematicians in order:

(a) according to the year in which they were born.

(b) according to their age when they died.

Draw a time line and place the mathematicians on it, using the dates shown in the table.

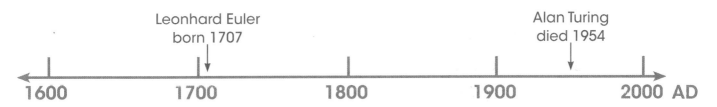

Find out about the work of these and other famous mathematicians.

Sequences (1)

Let's investigate

Use the clues to find the **sixth** number in this sequence.

- The fourth number is equal to 3 × 10.
- The second number is equal to 10 + 6.
- The third number is half way between the second and fourth numbers.
- The fifth number is 7 more than the fourth number.

Vocabulary

multiple: a number that can be divided exactly by another number is a multiple of that number. Start at 0 and count up in equal steps and you will find numbers that are multiples of the step size.

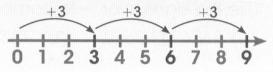

3, 6, 9, 12, ... are multiples of 3.

1 Identify the number sequences shown on these grids.

(a)

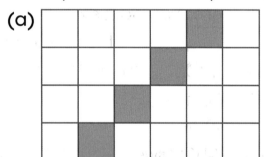

(b)

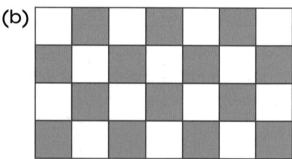

2 The grids at the top of page 7 have been torn so you can only see part of them.

(a) What multiples have been shaded?

(b) How wide might the grids be?

Grid 1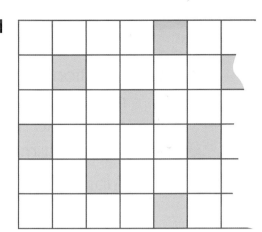

Grid 2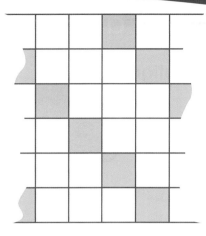

3   Fill in the missing numbers in these sequences.

(a) ?   ?   49   53   ?   61   ?   ?

(b) 98   107   ?   125   134   ?   ?

(c) ?   ?   ?   43   32   21   ?

What is the rule for each sequence?

4   This is an 8 by 8 number grid. Ask your teacher for a print out.

1	2	3	4	5	6	7	8
9	10	11	12	13	14	15	16
17	18	19	20	21	22	23	24
25	26	27	28	29	30	31	32
33	34	35	36	37	38	39	40
41	42	43	44	45	46	47	48
49	50	51	52	53	54	55	56
57	58	59	60	61	62	63	64

(a) On your copy of the grid, colour the multiples of 7.

(b) What do you notice?

(c) If you continued the sequence, would 100 be in the sequence?

(d) Is 105 in the sequence? How do you know?

Discuss your answers with a partner.

5   What is the next number in this sequence? How do you know?

8,   6,   4,   2,   0,   ...

6   A sequence starts at 400 and 70 is subtracted each time.

400,   330,   260,   ...

What are the first two numbers in the sequence that are less than zero?

Addition and subtraction (1)

Let's investigate

A: I will count on in hundreds from 3.

B: I will count on in tens from 903.

C: I will count back in thousands from 9003.

If all three children count at the same speed, who will say 1003 first?

Vocabulary

addition: to combine more than one number to make a total, or sum.

subtraction: to take away, or find the difference between numbers.

total: the result when numbers are added together.

difference: the result when a number is subtracted from another number.

1   Complete the number sequences to open the safe.

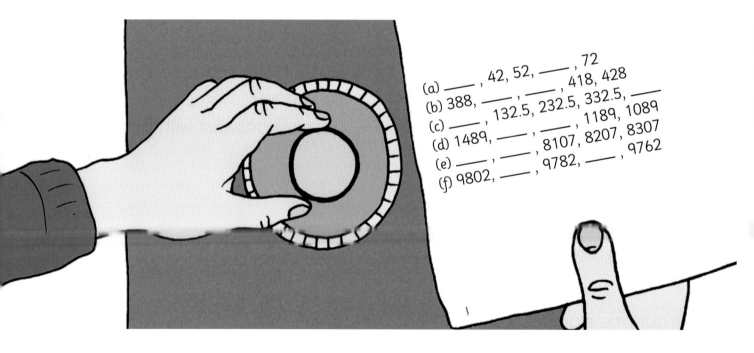

(a) ____ , 42, 52, ____ , 72

(b) 388, ____ , ____ , 418, 428

(c) ____ , 132.5, 232.5, 332.5, ____

(d) 1489, ____ , ____ , 1189, 1089

(e) ____ , ____ , 8107, 8207, 8307

(f) 9802, ____ , 9782, ____ , 9762

2 Put 578 into each of these machines and calculate
what value will come out.

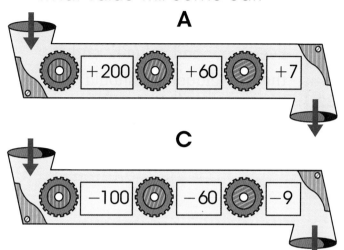

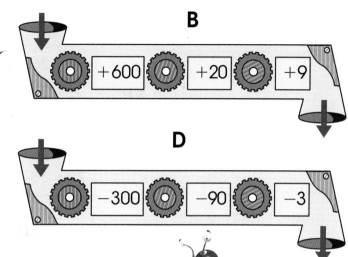

3 Pairs of numbers in this grid have
a difference of 439. Find the pair
of numbers that **do not** have a
difference of 439.

522	104	972	234
543	673	143	962
542	961	533	181
243	523	620	682

You might need to find all
the pairs first. Choose your own
method, always estimate first.
For example, 970 − 530 = 440;
therefore, 533 and 972 might be
a pair. We have added using
partitioning to check:

```
   533
+  439
   900  (500 + 400)
   960  (30 + 30)
   972  (3 + 9)
```

so 972 − 533 = 439; and so
972 and 533 is a pair.

4 Play this game with a partner.

You both choose two of the number cards in secret,
and find the total of the two numbers.

Tell your partner the total you made and challenge them
to find the two numbers you chose.

The first player to work out their partner's cards wins.

Adding more numbers

Let's investigate

This is a magic square.

Two of the numbers in this square have been swapped.

Find the two numbers and swap them back so that the magic square works.

40	26	27	37
29	35	31	32
33	34	30	36
28	38	39	25

Every row and column, and the two diagonals, should add up to 130.

1   Alyssa, Anish and Axel have been raising money by doing chores for four months.

    These graphs show how much they raised each month.

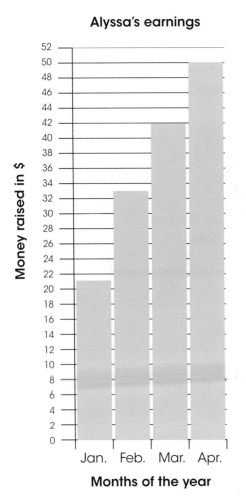

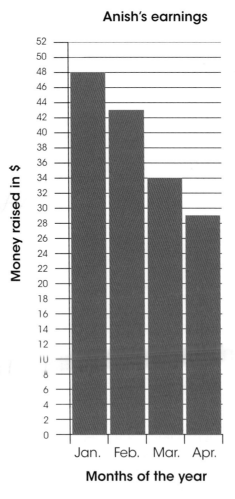

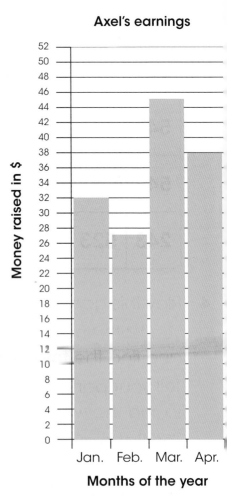

(a) Alyssa hoped to raise at least $140.
Did she reach her target?

(b) How much money did Axel raise?

(c) Who raised the most money in total?

(d) What was the total amount of money raised by all three children?

2   Anish, Alyssa and Axel's money was raised for a penguin rescue mission.
A disaster has occurred at Penguin Rock and the penguins need
to be rescued by boat.

Each boat can carry a maximum of 128 kg of penguins.
The table lists the penguin's masses.

Which penguins will you put together in the boats?
Try to use just three boats.

Penguin's name	Mass in kg
Percy	35
Petunia	34
Pablo	33
Petra	32
Prince	31
Pom	30
Petal	29
Pop	28
Preda	27
Pal	26
Penelope	25
Pan	24
Prentice	23

3   With a partner, discuss a strategy for finding the
total mass of all the penguins.

Work out the total mass of the penguins.

Turn the page for question 4.

4   Once all the penguins have been rescued, one last boat visits all the other rocks to check for penguins. The boat starts and finishes at Penguin Rock.

Plan a journey the boat can make so that it visits all the rocks. Then work out the distance the boat will travel.

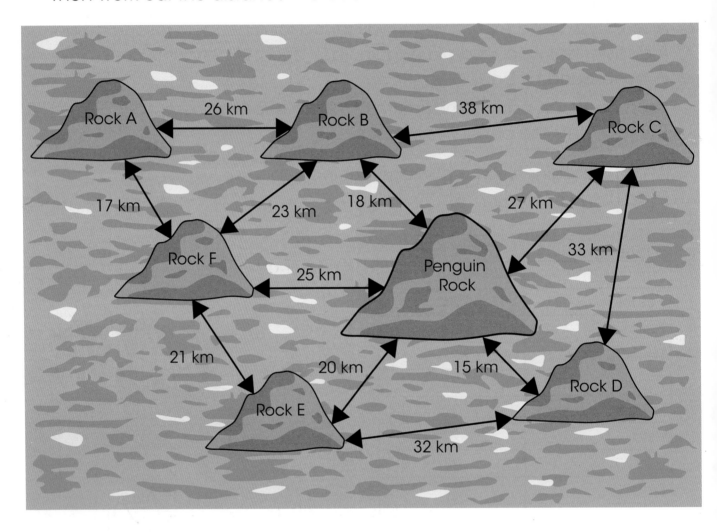

Vocabulary

operation: something you do to a number. $+ - \times \div$ are all mathematical operations.

inverse: having the opposite effect. $+9$ is the inverse of -9,

$\times 5$ is the inverse of $\div 5$.

inverse operations: operations that 'undo' each other if applied to a number one after the other. For example,

$$10 \left(-2 + 2 \right) = 10$$
$$7 \left(\times 3 \div 3 \right) = 7$$

Let's investigate

These numbers follow a pattern.

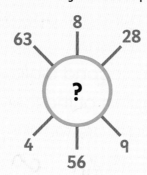

What number goes in the middle?

> Look at the numbers on each end of a line passing through the circle.

Knowing your times tables will help you to solve the following questions.

1   Sara is trying to find the code to unlock a treasure chest.

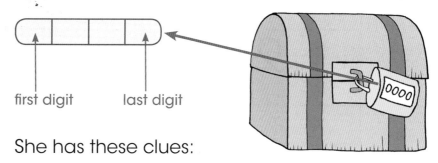

first digit   last digit

She has these clues:

- The last digit is $28 \div 7$.
- The sum of the middle two digits is 4.
- The first digit is double the last digit.
- All the digits are in the $2\times$ table.
- Two digits are multiples of 4.

What is the code number?

Turn the page for more questions.

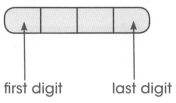

first digit   last digit

2   Cheng is trying to find the code number to unlock
    a different treasure chest.

    He has these clues:

    • The sum of the first and second digits is a multiple of 6.
    • The difference between the first and second digits is 6.
    • The sum of the third and fourth digits is the same as
      the sum of the first and second digits.
    • The first digit is the smallest of the four digits.
    • The third and fourth digits are the same.
    • There are no zeros in the code.

    What is the code number?

3   Copy and complete these multiplication grids.

(a)

×	3	7	9	4	2
5					
					12
					6
					16
					8

(b)

×	3				10
9					
		25			
			49		
6				36	
					100

(c)

×	4	7	9	8	3
3					
4					
6					
8					
9					

(d)

×	4	6	8	7	5
					45
				21	
			56		
		24			
	8				

4 Write the correct sign in each box. Choose from these signs: = < >

(a) 3×8 ? 5×5 (b) 6×4 ? 4×6

(c) 7×8 ? 6×9 (d) 4×4 ? 2×8

5 Here is part of a number grid.

27	28	29	30
37	38	39	40
47	48	49	50
57	58	59	60

Which numbers are multiples of 7?

6 Here are 10 digit cards.

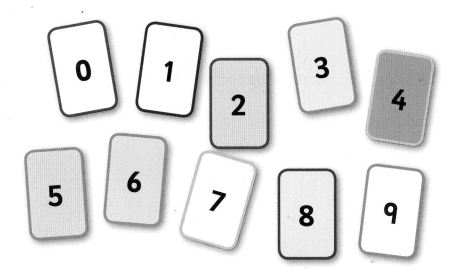

Use the cards to make five two-digit numbers that are multiples of 3.

You can use each card **only once**.

?	?		?	?		?	?		?	?		?	?

Written methods of multiplication

Let's investigate

The numbers in the triangles are connected by a rule.

121 **?** 3 = 363

Use the first triangle to find the rule.

Then use the rule to complete the other two triangles.

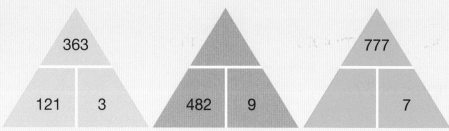

Vocabulary

product: the answer you get when you multiply two or more numbers together.

product

7 × 8 = 56

1 Estimate first, then calculate:

(a) 318 × 2   (b) 426 × 3   (c) 512 × 7

(d) 936 × 8   (e) 671 × 9   (f) 384 × 6

2 This example shows one method to caluclate 5.7 × 4

Estimate: 5.7 × 4 is approximately 6 × 4 = 24

×	5	0.7
4	20	2.8

20 + 2.8 = 22.8

22.8 is close to 24, so 22.8 is a reasonable answer.

Use this method, or any other method, to work out the following:

(a) 4.9 × 5   (b) 6.3 × 7   (c) 3.8 × 8

(d) 5.7 × 9   (e) 4.3 × 6   (f) 4.5 × 9

3 Calculate double 15.5

4 A packet contains 1.5 kg of rice.
   How much rice is in five packets?

5 A rectangle is made of squares with sides 3.2 centimetres long.

(a) What is the length of the rectangle?

(b) What is the width of the rectangle?

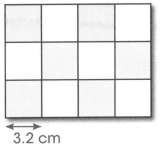

3.2 cm

6 Use only the digits 2, 5 and 7 to complete this calculation.

| ? | ? | × 3 = | ? | ? |

7 Use only the digits 1, 5 and 7 to complete this calculation.

| ? | ? | × 3 = | ? | ? | ? |

8 Write what the missing numbers could be.

| ? | × | ? | = 750

How many different answers can you find?

9 Here is a multiplication question:

| ? | ? | × | ? | =

(a) Use the digits 4, 6 and 8 to make the largest product.

(b) Use the digits 4, 6 and 8 to make the smallest product.

10 A, B, C and D each represent a different digit.

| A | B | B |

       | A | ×

_____

| C | D | D |

_____

What numbers do A, B, C and D represent?

More multiplication

Let's investigate

The top number in each pattern is the product of multiplying the two numbers in the middle blocks.

The bottom number in each pattern is the sum of the two middle blocks.

Find the missing numbers.

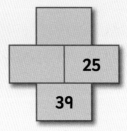

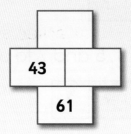

Start with a subtraction.

The example below uses the grid method to find the product of 39 and 15.

×	30	9
10	300	90
5	150	45

$450 + 135 = 585$

Remember to show all your working

1   Use any method to calculate:

    (a) 34×27 **(b)** 94×35 **(c)** 87×48

    (d) 26×56 **(e)** 58×63 **(f)** 74×42

2   Calculate 37×25.

    Discuss with your partner the most efficient way of working it out.

3   Use the digits 0, 2, 3 and 5 to complete this calculation.

4   Calculate 13×13 and 31×31. What do you notice about the results?

Written methods of division

Let's investigate

Use the digits 2, 5, 7 and 9 to make a correct calculation.

You must use each digit **only once**.

$$? \; ? \; ? \div ? = 136$$

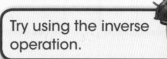

Try using the inverse operation.

The example below uses repeated subtraction to divide 124 by 5.

```
124
100 –   20 × 5
 24
 20 –    4 × 5
  4     24 × 5      so 124 ÷ 5 = 24 r 4
```

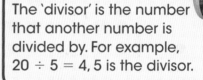

Remember to show all your working.

1 Estimate first, then calculate:

   (a) 336 ÷ 7   **(b)** 387 ÷ 9   **(c)** 444 ÷ 6

   (d) 392 ÷ 8   **(e)** 332 ÷ 4   **(f)** 406 ÷ 7

2 Estimate first, then calculate:

   (a) 567 ÷ 5   **(b)** 396 ÷ 7   **(c)** 515 ÷ 9

The 'divisor' is the number that another number is divided by. For example, 20 ÷ 5 = 4, 5 is the divisor.

3 What is the missing number?

   160 ÷ ? = 8

4 Hamid has 104 stickers. He has 8 pages in his sticker album.
   He places the same number of stickers on each page.
   How many stickers does Hamid place on each page?

5 Plants are sold in trays.
   Each tray holds 12 plants.
   Fatima needs 160 plants for her garden.
   How many trays must Fatima buy?

Multiples and squares

Let's investigate

15 multiplied by itself gives a three-digit number.

| 1 | 5 | × | 1 | 5 | = | 2 | 2 | 5 |

What is the **largest** two-digit number that can be multiplied by itself to give a three-digit number?

| ? | ? | × | ? | ? | = | ? | ? | ? |

> Think about square numbers.

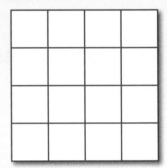

Vocabulary

square number: the number you get when you multiply a whole number by itself.

For example, 4 × 4 = 16

16 is a square number.

1   These patterns of dots show the first four square numbers.

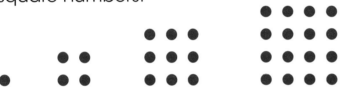

Draw a dot pattern for the fifth square number.

2   Look at these numbers.
    Write down the numbers which are:

    14   35   30   90
         100   7   21
      9
    24   64   16   25   36

    (a) multiples of 6.
    (b) multiples of 7.
    (c) square numbers.

3   Copy the sorting diagram. Write a number between 50 and 100 in each space.

	square number	not a square number
even number		
not an even number		

4   Use the digits 1, 2, 5 and 7 to complete these statements.
    You can use each digit as many times as you like.

    | ? | ? | is a multiple of 3.

    | ? | ? | is a multiple of 9.

    | ? | ? | is a square number.

5   This sequence shows multiples of 4:

    4, 8, 12, 16, 20, …

    Will 114 be in the sequence?

    Explain how you know.

6   Find two **square numbers** to make each of these calculations correct.

    (a) ? + ? = 10   (b) ? + ? = 20
    (c) ? + ? = 40   (d) ? + ? = 50
    (e) ? + ? = 80   (f) ? + ? = 90
    (g) ? + ? = 100

7   Solve these number riddles.

    (a) The number is:
        • a square number
        • a multiple of 3
        • less than 25.

    (b) The number is:
        • a square number
        • an even number
        • a single-digit number.

    (c) The number is:
        • a two-digit number less than 30
        • a multiple of 4
        • a multiple of 5.

Tests of divisibility

Let's investigate

Which of these numbers is divisible by 5 but **not** by 2 or 10?

250   205   502   520

Explain to your partner how you know.

Write down two more numbers that are divisible by 5 but not by 2 or 10.

Vocabulary

divisible: can be divided without a remainder.

test of divisibility: a number can be divided by …

2 if the last digit is divisable by 2.

5 if the last digit is 5 or 0.

10 if the last digit is 0.

100 if the last two digits are 00.

1   Look at this set of numbers.

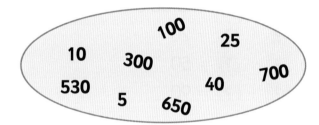

Write down:

(a) the numbers that are divisible by 100.

(b) the numbers that are divisible by 10.

(c) the numbers that are divisible by 5.

Discuss your results with a partner.

2   Write down the numbers from the list below that are divisible by 2:

13   42   63   21   48   84   6

How do you know they are divisible by 2?

3   Pair these numbers so that the difference between each pair is divisible by 5. The first one has been done for you:

74 − 39 = 35 and 35 is divisible by 5

48   89   ⑦④   66   23   ㉛⑨   64   91

4 (a) Write down a number which is divisible by 5 and 10.

   (b) Write down a number which is divisible by 2 and 5.

5 Ask your teacher for a print out of the grid below.

   Shade each number that is divisible by 2, 5 or 10, on your grid.

1	70	20	80	3	13	60	17	43	52	54	90	31
27	4	63	32	69	39	44	19	29	75	9	14	59
67	62	46	10	53	22	70	25	7	12	28	55	73
63	8	17	34	29	77	32	71	43	59	49	62	79
41	30	38	34	73	33	50	51	69	53	57	105	87

   What is the answer to the secret calculation?

   Devise a similar puzzle, then ask your partner to solve it.

6 Using all the digits 0, 1, 5 and 6:

   (a) find the largest odd number divisible by 5.

   (b) find the smallest number, greater than 1000, that is divisible by 5.

7 Vincent is making a number sentence using the digits 1, 3 and 5.

   What are the missing digits?

   | ? | ? | × 5 = | ? | ? | ? |

Factors

Let's investigate

Find three different factors of 12 that will give a total of 12 when added together.

$\boxed{?} + \boxed{?} + \boxed{?} = 12$

Find four different factors of 12 that total 12.

$\boxed{?} + \boxed{?} + \boxed{?} + \boxed{?} = 12$

Write down all the factors of 12.

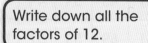

Vocabulary

factor: a whole number that divides into another number without a remainder.

For example,
$6 \div 2 = 3$ and
$6 \div 3 = 2$
so, 2 and 3 are factors of 6

$$\mathbf{2 \times 3 = 6}$$

factor   factor

1   This is a factor bug for 24.

Draw a factor bug for:

(a) 12

(b) 32

(c) 16

What do you notice about the factor bug for 16?

2 Which of these numbers are factors of 42?

2   3   4   5   6   7

3 2 is a factor of both 12 and 18.

Write down two more numbers greater than 1 that are factors of both 12 and 18.

4 The number 8 has four factors: 1, 2, 4 and 8.

Find a different single-digit number that has exactly four factors.

5 Write down two factors of 24 that total 11.

Geometry

Parallel and perpendicular

Let's investigate

Shweta draws two pairs of lines.

One pair are parallel and the other pair are perpendicular.

parallel   perpendicular

Check Shweta's lines. Are they correct?

How could she draw them more accurately?

1 Look around you.

Describe five pairs of **parallel lines** that you can see. Use a ruler to check that the distance between the lines is always the same.

Describe five pairs of **perpendicular lines** that you can see. Use a right-angle checker to check that the lines meet at 90°.

Vocabulary

parallel: lines that are always the same distance apart. ═══

perpendicular: lines that intersect (cross over) at right angles.

right angle: an angle measuring 90°.

Making a right-angle checker
1. Take a piece of paper (any shape).
2. Fold the paper as shown here.

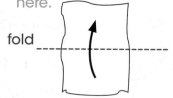
fold

3. Then fold the paper in the opposite direction.

4. The new corner made by the two folds is a right angle.

right angle

2　Which of the letters below have pairs of parallel lines?

A B C D E F G H I J K L M N O P Q R S T U V W X Y Z

3　**Tartan** is a pattern of perpendicular and parallel lines.
There is a set of coloured threads in one direction,
and another set of coloured threads cross at a right angle.
Look at these tartan designs.

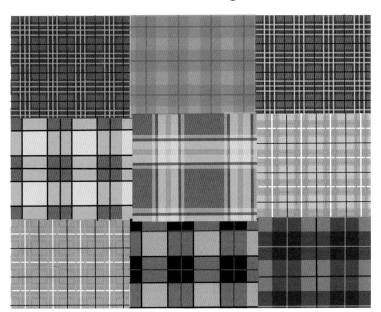

Scottish and Irish kilts are made from tartan. In North America tartan is often called plaid.

How do you think some of the designs were made?
Discuss with your partner.

4　Choose one of the tartan designs above.

Copy the design using colouring pencils, or make it using coloured strips of paper. You will need a ruler and a right-angle checker.

Check that your parallel lines are parallel by measuring the gap between the lines at different points to make sure they are always the same distance apart.

Make sure your perpendicular lines meet at a right angle using your right-angle checker.

Ask your partner to check that your tartan has pairs of lines that are parallel and perpendicular.

Triangles

Let's investigate

Surita has made a triangle using a length of string.

> My triangle is equilateral. I measured one side. It is 4 cm long.

How long is her piece of string?

George has made a triangle using a different length of string.

How long could his piece of string be?

> My triangle is isosceles. I measured two sides. One is 4 cm and one is 5 cm.

> There is more than one answer.

1   The noticeboard on the opposite page has been divided into 12 sections labeled A to L.

Each section contains a set of three pins. Imagine joining these pins using three straight lines.

Which sets of pins will make:

- an equilateral triangle?
- a scalene triangle?
- an isosceles triangle?

Do any sets of pins **not** make a triangle?

Vocabulary

equilateral triangle: a triangle with all angles equal and all sides equal.

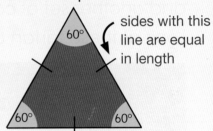

sides with this line are equal in length

60°   60°   60°

isosceles triangle: a triangle with two angles equal and two sides equal.

scalene triangle: a triangle with no angles equal and no sides equal.

right-angled triangle: a triangle where one of the angles is a right angle.

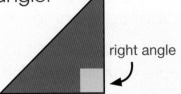

right angle

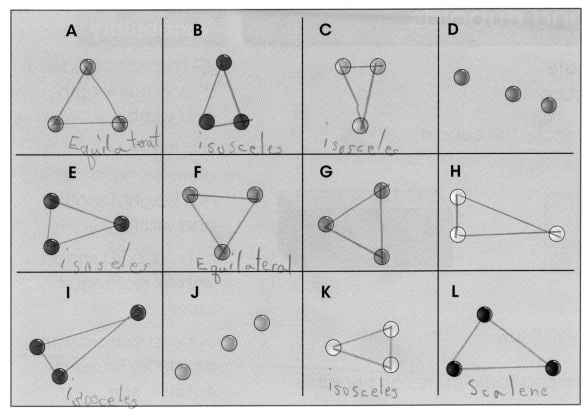

The grid cells contain the following handwritten labels:

- A: Equilateral
- B: isosceles
- C: isosceles
- E: isosceles
- F: Equilateral
- I: isosceles
- K: isosceles
- L: Scalene

2 (a) How many equilateral triangles can you find in this diagram?

   (b) Can you find any triangles in the diagram that are **not** equilateral?

   (c) Mark used 15 cm of string to make one of the small triangles in the diagram. What length of string does he need to make the largest triangle?

3 Who is correct?

A — All triangles have 3 sides.

E — None of the sides of a scalene triangle are the same length.

B — The two sides that are the same length in an isosceles triangle are longer than the other side.

C — A triangle can be isosceles and right-angled.

D — All triangles have three lines of reflective symmetry.

Cubes and cuboids

Let's investigate
Look at this cuboid.

Does this net make the cuboid?

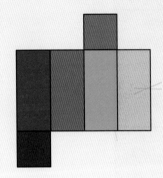 

Explain how you know.

1   Marie arranged some cubes on her table.

Below are four drawings of cubes on a table from different sides. Two of the pictures show Marie's arrangement but from different views. Which are the pictures of Marie's cubes?

A   B   C   D

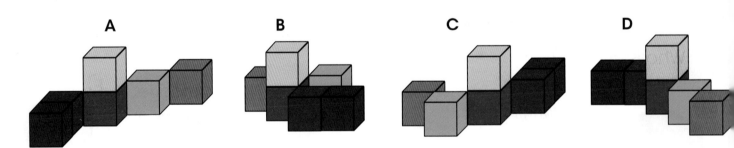

2   Make your own arrangement of cubes.
    Draw a picture of your arrangement.

3   Ask a partner to copy your arrangement of cubes using only your picture.

4. Which of these nets would make a closed cube?

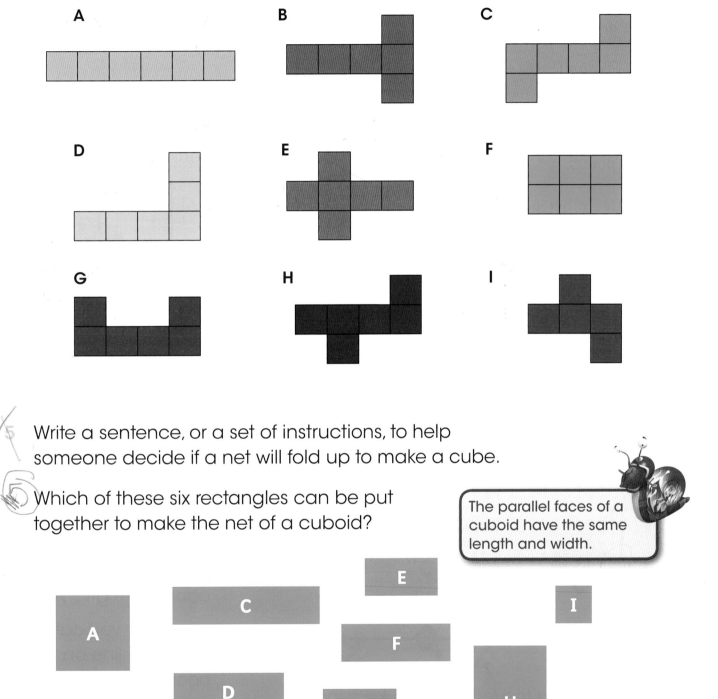

5. Write a sentence, or a set of instructions, to help someone decide if a net will fold up to make a cube.

6. Which of these six rectangles can be put together to make the net of a cuboid?

The parallel faces of a cuboid have the same length and width.

Coordinates

Let's investigate

Draw a grid like this.

Plot (1, 0) and (5, 4) on your grid.

Draw a line between the two points.

What three other pairs of coordinates are on the line?

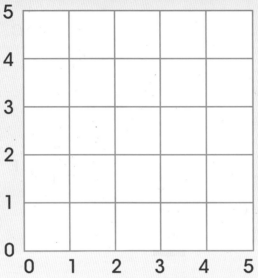

Vocabulary

coordinates: a pair of numbers that show position on a grid.

For example, (3, 2) means 3 across horizontally and 2 up vertically.

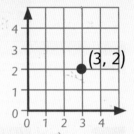

plot: to mark points on a grid using coordinates.

horizontal: parallel to the horizon. _____

vertical: perpendicular to the horizon.

x-axis: the horizontal reference line on a coordinate grid. ⊢⟶

y-axis: the vertical reference line on a coordinate grid.

1. You need four keys to open the treasure chest. The first three keys are at the coordinates (4, 2), (2, 0) and (1, 1).

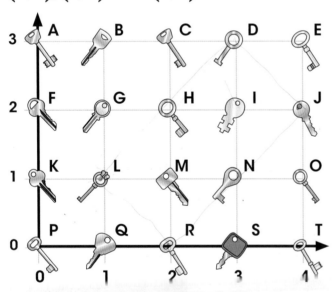

(a) What are the letters of the keys that open the first three locks? R, L, J

(b) The four keys that open the chest are at the corners of a rectangle. Which key opens the fourth lock? O

(c) What are the coordinates of the fourth key?
(3, 3)

4   Each set of coordinates makes a triangle.

(a) A (6, 8) (7, 4) (8, 8)

     B (1, 1) (6, 1) (6, 4)

     C (4, 2) (6, 6) (8, 2)

     D (3, 5) (4, 7) (7, 7)

     E (3, 4) (1, 6) (5, 6)

     Work out which type of triangle
     each set of coordinates makes.
     Triangle A is shown on the grid.

(b) Copy and complete the
     Venn diagram.

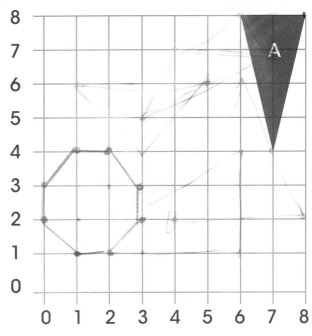

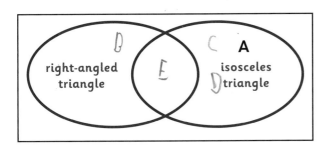

     Put the letter for each triangle in the correct part of the diagram.
     Triangle A has been done for you.

5   Write a set of three coordinates that do **not** make a triangle. (1,3)(2,3)(3,3)

6   With a partner, investigate
    sets of three coordinates
    that do **not** make a triangle.

    Describe what you find out.

Translation and reflection

Let's investigate

Which of these is the missing piece from the wrapping paper? Explain how you know.

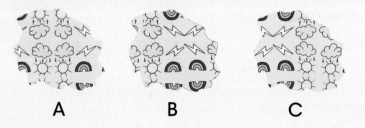

A   B   C

translation: moving an object or image in a straight line without rotating it. For example,

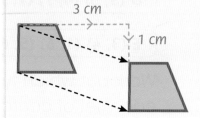

reflection: making a mirror image by flipping an object in a mirror line without rotating it. For example,

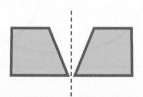

1   The pattern below is made on a grid of centimetre squares.

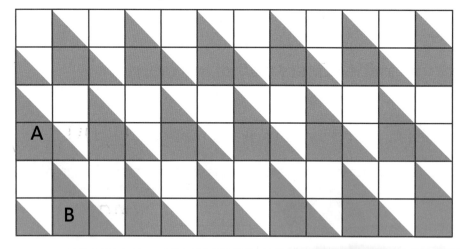

(a) Look at the middle row of triangles.
   Each triangle is translated right to make the pattern.
   How many centimetres is each triangle translated to the right?

(b) Describe the translation that moves triangle A to triangle B.

2   Create your own pattern by translating one shape on centimetre squared paper. Make sure the shape is bigger than one square on the paper.
    Write instructions for how the shape in your pattern is translated.

3   Find a path through the grid to the bottom row. Start at a kite in the top row.
    You can move to a next door kite if it is a reflection of the kite you are on.
    The kite can be a reflection in a horizontal or vertical mirror line.

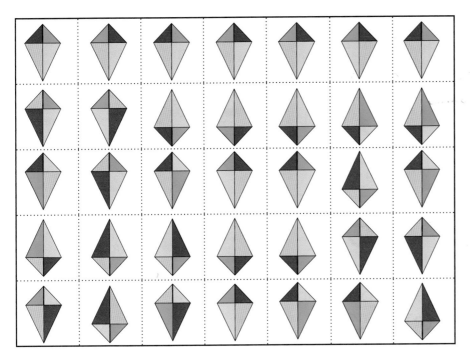

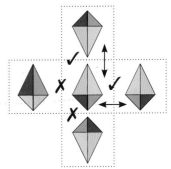

4   Copy the coloured lines, shapes and mirror line onto square paper.

    Reflect each of the coloured lines and shapes in the mirror line.

Each part of the line or shape is reflected in the mirror line.

The reflection is the same distance from the mirror line as the original picture, but on the other side.

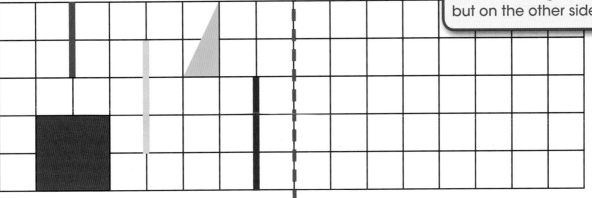

Measure

Mass

Let's investigate

Cheryl visits her grandfather for his birthday.

Her hand luggage has a total mass of 4.8 kg.

Which of these objects are in her bag?

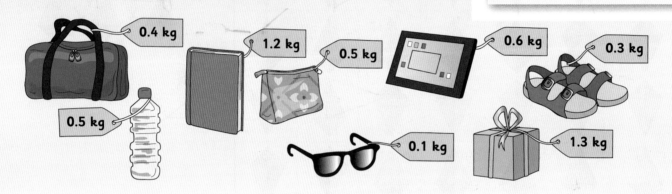

0.4 kg   1.2 kg   0.5 kg   0.6 kg   0.3 kg   0.5 kg   0.1 kg   1.3 kg

1   Write down the mass of each parcel in grams.

(a)

(b)

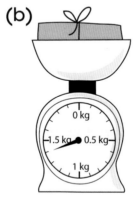

(c)

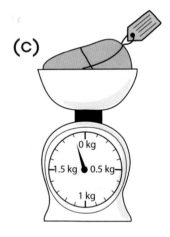

(d)

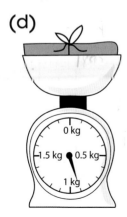

(e)

(f)

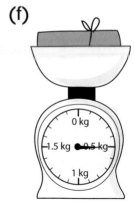

2 Suntia has lots of parcels to send.

(a) Put the parcels in order from lightest to heaviest.

(b) How much would each parcel cost to post?

3 Class 5 have been measuring out flour for a cookery lesson.
Each learner started with a 2 kg bag of flour.
How much flour is left in each child's bag?
Write your answer in grams.

Telling the time

Let's investigate

These are 24-hour digital clocks.

The digit '3' appears in these examples twice.

Which digit from 0 to 9 is used for the most times on a clock in 24 hours?

> Start by working out which digit can be in each of the four positions **?** **?** : **?** **?**.
> Then think about how many times these digits can be in each position.

Vocabulary

12-hour clock: one day is divided into two 12-hour periods, am and pm.

24-hour clock: one day is divided into one 24-hour period.

analogue: a time shown on a clock with hands.

digital: a time shown on a clock with digits.

am: ante meridiem, a time between midnight and midday (noon).

pm: post meridiem, a time between midday (noon) and midnight.

---

1 Look at these digits.

1   0   8   5

(a) Use these digits to make the earliest time in the day on a 24-hour clock.
01.58

(b) Use these digits to make the latest time in the day on a 24-hour clock.
1890

2 Change these 12-hour clock times to 24-hour clock times.

(a) 6:28 am 6:28   (b) 1:37 pm 13:37
(c) 4:04 pm 16:04 (d) 5:45 am 5:45
(e) 11:53 pm 23:53 (f) 7:28 pm 19:28
(g) 12:32 pm 00:32 (h) 12:16 am 00:16

3 The minute hand has fallen off the clocks in these pictures.

Estimate the time in each picture.

Write your estimate using 24-hour digital clock notation.

4 The numbers on a digital clock are made using seven little lights.

There are 28 little lights in total.

This clock is running out of power.

Only 14 of the lights work at any time!

It shows 17 minutes past 9 in the evening, using 12 lights.

Which of these times could be shown correctly on this clock with just 14 lights?

(a) a quarter past six in the morning.

(b) twenty-one minutes past five in the evening.

(c) five minutes to eight in the morning.

(d) half past seven in the morning.

(e) thirteen minutes to ten at night.

(f) twenty-one minutes past nine in the evening.

Timetables

Let's investigate

Lucia's little brother has scribbled on her timetable!
Work out the missing times for buses B and C.

> Every bus takes the same amount of time to reach each destination.

	Bus A	Bus B	Bus C	Bus D
Village	11:51	12:48		14:42
Town	12:08			14:59
City	12:32		14:26	15:23
Harbour	12:47	13:	14:41	15:38

1   The Fernandes family are visiting the city for the **weekend**. These leaflets show what attractions are taking place.

> Read all the information.

(a) On what day, date and time will the family be able to see the parachute display team?

(b) What time should the family be at the art gallery to join the Kids art club?

(c) At what time will the family be able to feed the giraffes?

(d) The acrobatic display on Sunday lasts 25 minutes. If the family watch it, how long will they have to get to the temporary art exhibition tour?

2   Use the leaflets to plan a weekend for the family.

The City Zoo

Weekdays

1000	Elephant feed
1130	Falconry display
1200	Giraffe feed
1315	Sea lion feed
1530	Meet the keepers

Weekends

1000	Elephant feeds
1130	Falconry display
1215	Giraffe feed
1345	Sea lion feed
1630	Meet the keepers

The Annual City Airshow
14–15 May

Saturday

1100	Fast jets 1
1120	1950s aeroplanes
1145	Helicopter display
1210	Pre-1940 aeroplanes
1300	Wing walkers
1330	Fast jets 2
1350	Acrobatic display team

Sunday

1210	Fast jets 1
1330	1950s aeroplanes
1255	Helicopter display
1320	Parachute display team
1410	Wing walkers
1440	Fast jets 2
1500	Acrobatic display team

The National Art Gallery

weekdays

1145	Modern galleries tour
1300	16th Century art tour
1530	Drawing studio
1600	Kid's art club
1730	Gallery closes

weekends

1215	Modern galleries tour
1325	Kid's art club
1430	16th Centruy art tour
1515	Kid's art club
1630	Temporary art exhibition tour
1800	Gallery closes

Kid's Art Club

3 Use the timetable to answer questions 3 to 5.

Train timetable			
	A	**B**	**C**
Ourtown	10:11	12:32	14:23
Riverton	10:47	13:08	14:59
Hillbury	11:17	13:38	15:29
Newcity	12:32	14:53	16:44

When the interval is more than 60 minutes, record it as hours and minutes. For example, 75 minutes = 1 hour and 15 minutes.

How long does it take for the train to travel:

(a) from Ourtown to Riverton?

(b) from Hillbury to Newcity?

(c) from Ourtown to Hillbury?

(d) from Ourtown to Newcity?

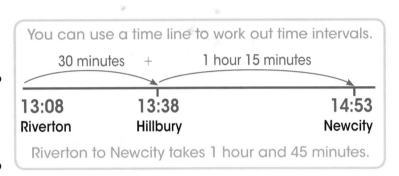

You can use a time line to work out time intervals.

30 minutes + 1 hour 15 minutes

13:08 — **13:38** — **14:53**
Riverton — Hillbury — Newcity

Riverton to Newcity takes 1 hour and 45 minutes.

4 How long would I have to wait for a train if I arrived at:

(a) Ourtown station at 9:42? (b) Riverton station at 10:58?

(c) Hillbury station at 13:17? (d) Riverton station at 14:36?

5 Which is the latest train I can catch from Ourtown to arrive at:

(a) Riverton station by 12:00? (b) Hillbury station by 14:15?

(c) Newcity station by 15:30? (d) Hillbury station by 15:40?

Area (1)

Let's investigate

I made a rectangle out of centimetre squares. It has an area of 40 cm². How many rows of squares did I use?

Which of Safwan's classmates cannot be correct?

Vocabulary

square centimetre (cm²): a unit used to measure the area of a surface. A square with side length 1 cm has an area of 1 cm².

1 cm | 1 cm²
1 cm

Safwan's rectangle has 5 rows of squares.
– Aileen

Safwan's rectangle has 8 rows of squares.
– Willow

Safwan's rectangle has 2 rows of squares.
– Dominique

Safwan's rectangle has 10 rows of squares.
– Ekene

Safwan's rectangle has 7 rows of squares.
– Senbi

1 Each learner uses 1 cm² squares to make a rectangle.

(a) What is the area of each rectangle described by the children?

A
My rectangle has 5 rows of 6 squares.

D
My rectangle has 10 rows of 6 squares.

B
My rectangle has 9 rows of 3 square centimetres.

E
My rectangle has 7 rows of 8 squares.

C
My rectangle has 4 rows of 4 squares.

F
My rectangle has 12 rows of 5 squares.

(b) Draw each rectangle on centimetre squared paper to check that your answers are correct.

2 The coordinate grid shows positions in a stream.
   Each square has an area of 1 cm² and contains some nuggets of gold.

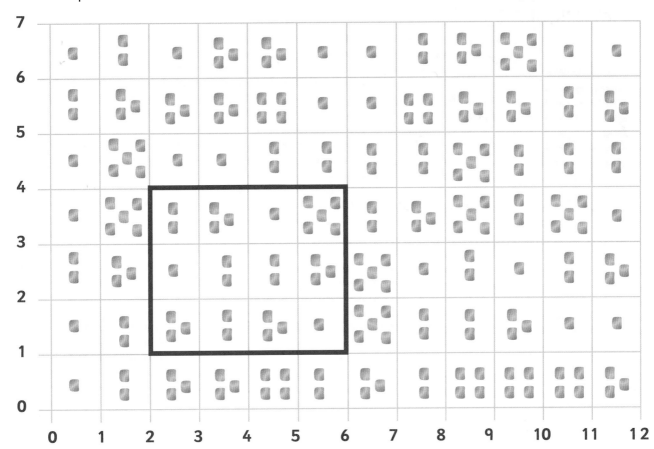

You can collect nuggets of gold by making
a rectangle anywhere on the grid using
the coordinates of the four corners.

The red rectangle has 3 rows
of 4 squares so it has an area
of 12 cm². The coordinates of its
corners are (2, 1), (6, 1), (2, 4)
and (6, 4).
There are 28 nuggets of gold in
this rectangle.

(a) What is the area of the rectangle with
    corner coordinates (0, 0), (0, 1), (12, 0)
    and (12, 1)?

(b) How many gold nuggets are in the rectangle with corner coordinates
    (6, 3), (6, 5), (12, 3), (12, 5)?

(c) Write the corner coordinates of a rectangle of 12 cm² that collects
    27 gold nuggets.

(d) Write the corner coordinates of a rectangle of 12 cm² that collects
    37 gold nuggets.

(e) Write the corner coordinates and area of a rectangle that collects
    11 gold nuggets.

Perimeter (1)

Let's investigate

I am thinking of a shape. The sides are all 12 cm long and the perimeter is 60 cm. What is my shape?

1   All of these shapes are regular polygons. What is the perimeter of each shape?

(a)

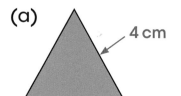

4 cm

(b)

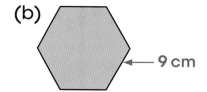

9 cm

(c)

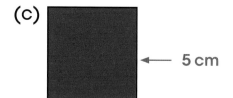

5 cm

(d)

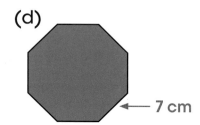

7 cm

(e)

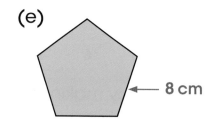

8 cm

(f)

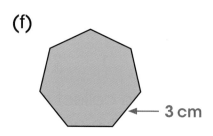

3 cm

2   All of these shapes are regular polygons. What is the length of each side?

(a)

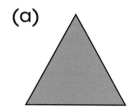

porimeter = 10 cm

(b)

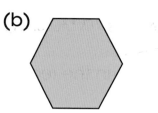

perimeter = 36 cm

(c)

perimeter = 32 cm

(d)

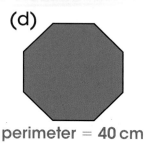

perimeter = 40 cm

(e)

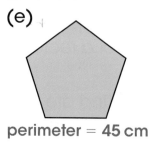

perimeter = 45 cm

(f)

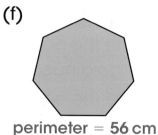

perimeter = 56 cm

3 A square with sides 6cm long has a perimeter of 24cm.
Describe two more regular polygons that have a
perimeter of 24cm.

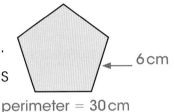

6cm

6cm
perimeter = 24cm

4 A regular pentagon with sides
6cm long has a perimeter of 30cm.
Describe two more regular polygons
that have a perimeter of 30cm.

6cm

perimeter = 30cm

5 Farmer Herlief, Farmer Dee and Farmer Lev need to walk around
the perimeter of their fences to check for damage.

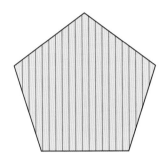

Farmer Herlief has a field shaped like a regular pentagon.
Each side is 25 metres long.

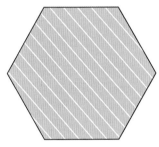

Farmer Dee has a field shaped like a regular hexagon.
Each side is 22 metres long.

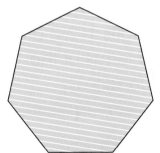

Farmer Lev has a field shaped like a regular heptagon.
Each side is 19 metres long.

Split the problem
into steps. You
could work out the
perimeter of each
field first.

It is  when they start checking their fences.

(a) It takes one minute to check 1 metre of fence.
What time will each farmer finish checking their fences?

(b) Will any farmers finish before half past three in the afternoon?

45

Number

Sequences (2)

Let's investigate

These worms have consecutive numbers in the circles.

The numbers add up to the number in the square.

①②③④⑤ ▣**15**

Complete these worms:

⚫⚫⚫ ▣**27**

⚫⚫⚫⚫⚫ ▣**25**

Describe to a partner how you can find the middle number of each worm.

1 Look at this sequence.
   Count the squares in each row of the staircase.

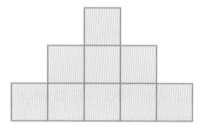

(a) Copy and complete the table below.

Number of rows	1	2	3	4	5	6
Number of squares in the bottom row	1	3	5			

(b) Continue the sequence to show your results.

1, 3, 5, ?, ?, ?, ?, ?, ?

(c) What do you know about these numbers? Tell your partner.

consecutive numbers: increase from smallest to largest one after the other, without any gaps. For example, 1, 2, 3 ,4 …

sequence: a list or pattern of numbers arranged according to a rule. For example, 4, 8, 16, 24 … is a sequence that starts at 4 with a rule of 'multiply by 2'.

term: part of a sequence separated by commas.
For example, in the sequence 1, 2, 3, 4, … the digits 1, 2, 3 and 4 are terms of the sequence.

2 Look at these staircases.

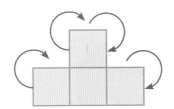
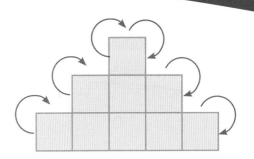

It takes 2 steps to go up and down.

It takes 4 steps to go up and down.

Continue the sequence 2, 4, ... What do you notice?

3 Look at this pattern of numbers.
It is known as Pascal's Triangle.

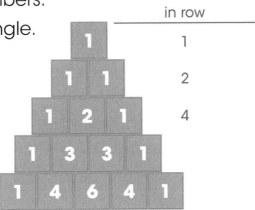

Sum of numbers in row

1

2

4

(a) How does the pattern continue to create the next row?
Discuss with a partner then draw the next two rows of the triangle.

(b) The sum of the numbers in each row is a sequence.
Find the sum of each row and write down the first eight numbers in the sequence.

1, 2, 4, ? , ? , ? , ? , ?

Describe the sequence.

(c) Look for other patterns in Pascal's Triangle. Write about your findings.

4 In this sequence every number is double the previous number.
What are the missing numbers?

? , ? 3, 6, 12, 24, 48, ?

5 What is the missing number in this sequence?

1, 3, 6, 10, ?

Explain how you worked it out.

General statements

t

Vocabulary

general statement: a statement that is not about particular examples and it is a rule that always works. For example, 'Two odd numbers added together give an even number'.

counter-example: an example that shows a general staement is wrong.

Let's investigate

Dinesh says:

I add three odd numbers and my answer is 50.

Is Dinesh correct?

Explain to a partner how you know.

1 Read these general statements.

   1 To multiply a number by 10, every digit moves one place to the left.

   2 To divide a number by 100, every digit moves two places to the right.

   3 To multiply a number by 1000, every digit moves three places to the left.

   Work with a partner to find examples for each statement. Discuss your answers, then write them down. Use a place value chart to help explain your answers.

Hundred thousand	Ten thousand	Thousand	Hundred	Ten	Unit
HTh	TTh	Th	H	T	U

2 Is the following a general statement?

   Every multiple of 5 ends in 5.

   Explain how you know.

3

When you add 5 to any number the answer will be odd.

Is Salem correct?

Explain how you know.

Vocabulary

positive number:
a number that is
greater than zero.

negative number: a
number that is less
than zero. We use a
(−) sign to show a
negative number.

```
  negative    positive
  numbers     numbers
←──────────┼──────────→
           0
```

Let's investigate

The coldest place where humans live is the Siberian village of Oymyakon.

On 6 February 1933, the temperature fell to −67.7 °C. This is the lowest temperature ever recorded outside Antarctica!

Investigate the temperature in different places around the world. List the temperatures in order, starting with the coldest.

1 Look at the thermometer.
   Which numbers are represented by the boxes?

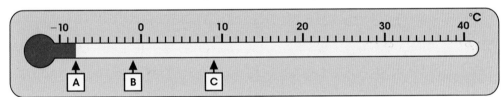

2 Here are some temperatures recorded in different places on the same day.
   7 °C   −2 °C   9 °C   −8 °C   0 °C   −9 °C   5 °C   −1 °C
   Draw a number line from −10 to 10 then mark the temperatures on your number line.

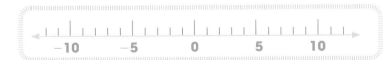

3 Write each of these sets of temperatures in order, starting with the coldest temperature:
   (a) 0 °C   −9 °C   3 °C   −2 °C
   (b) 3 °C   −4 °C   7 °C   −8 °C
   (c) −2 °C   2 °C   7 °C   −11 °C

Turn the page for more questions.

4   The temperature in England is 11 °C.
    The temperature in Iceland is 15 °C colder.
    What is the temperature in Iceland?

5   What is the missing number on this number line?

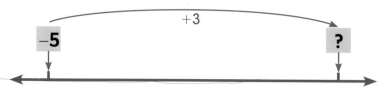

6   Calculate the new temperature.

    (a) The temperature is 8 °C and it cools down by 9 °C.

    (b) The temperature is 5 °C and it cools down by 5 °C.

    (c) The temperature is −2 °C and it cools down by 13 °C.

7   Write these temperature changes as number sentences:

    (a) −5 °C rises by 3 °C

    (b) 5 °C cools by 7 °C

    (c) −4 °C cools by 7 °C

8   The difference between the two numbers in the boxes is 10.

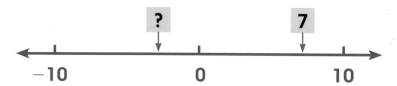

    What number goes in the empty box?

9   Here is part of a number line.
    What numbers go in the two empty boxes?

Vocabulary

tenth: a tenth is 1 part in 10 ($\frac{1}{10}$) of a whole and can be written as 0.1

H	T	U •	t
		0 •	1

hundredth: a hundredth is 1 part in 100 ($\frac{1}{100}$) and can be written as 0.01

H	T	U •	t	h
		0 •	0	1

The decimal system

Let's investigate

Join the dots to make a word.

Start with the smallest decimal and continue in order of size.

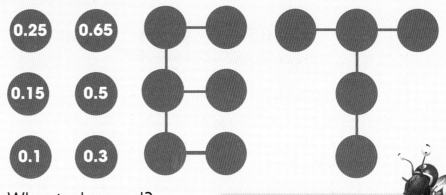

0.25	0.65
0.15	0.5
0.1	0.3

What is the word?

Write down all the decimals so they have two decimal places, then put them in order.

1   Write down the value of the digit 3 in each of these numbers:

(a) 72.3   (b) 84.03   (c) 5.53

2   Write these numbers in figures:

(a) fifteen point three seven

(b) one hundred and five point zero five

(c) thirty-four point three four

3   Sonia has these four cards:

She makes a number using all the cards.

What is the smallest number she can make that is greater than 1?

4 **(a)** Write these five numbers in a place value chart.

| 0.7 | 0.13 | 0.4 | 0.08 | 0.67 |

H	T	U	•	t	h
		0	•	7	

The first one has been done for you.

(b) Which of the five numbers are greater than 0.5?

5 Write these prices in order of size, starting with the smallest.

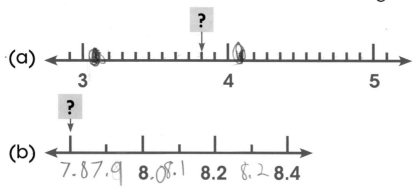

$35 $30·05 $3·50 $30·50

6 Look at these number lines. What number goes in each box?

(a)

?

3   4   5

(b)

?

7.8 7.9   8.0 8.1   8.2   8.3 8.4

7 Write the correct sign > or < between each pair of numbers.

(a) 3.4 **?** 3.04   **(b)** 4.5 **?** 4.55   *Not seven*
(c) 3.83 **?** 3.38   **(d)** 1.14 **?** 1.2   *If can*

8 Round these numbers to the nearest whole number.

(a) 4.6   **(b)** 4.55   **(c)** 4.45

.5 or up – round up   4 or under – round down

9 Here are four cards:

1   2   3   4

Use each card **once** to complete the statements below.

4 . **?** > **?** . 9

4 . **?** < **?** . 9

For Friday

H/w

Decimal facts

Let's investigate

Copy the diagram below.

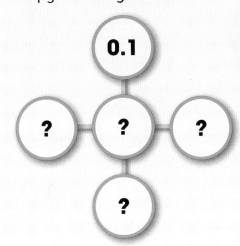

Place the numbers 0.2, 0.3, 0.4 and 0.5 in the circles so that the total down and across is 1.

1. Find the missing numbers.

   (a) $0.7 + ? = 1$ (b) $0.6 + ? = 1$ (c) $1 - ? = 0.3$

2. Find the missing numbers.

   (a) $5.3 + ? = 10$ (b) $? + 0.7 = 10$ (c) $10 - ? = 3.9$

3. (a) Find three numbers that total 1.

   $? . ? + ? . ? + ? . ? = 1$

   (b) Find three numbers that total 10.

   $? . ? + ? . ? + ? . ? = 10$

4. (a) What is the total of 0.6 and 0.4?
   (b) What is the difference between 1 and 0.9?
   (c) Find the sum of 5.4 and 4.6
   (d) Subtract 5.6 from 10.

5. Copy the diagram. Write a number in each circle so that the numbers along each side of the square have the same total.

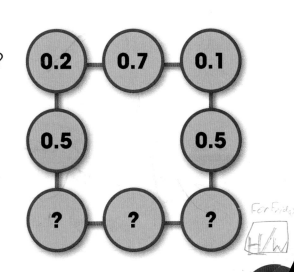

Multiplication strategies

Let's investigate

Here are some number cards.

Use four number cards to complete a 2 by 2 grid. Multiply the numbers on each row.

Example:

2	3
6	4

$2 \times 3 = 6$

$6 \times 4 = 24$

Move the cards around and multiply again. How many different products can you find?

Investigate with four different number cards.

1 Ingrid is using a multiplication grid to calculate the 8× table. She starts by writing the 2× table, then doubles and doubles again.

Number	1	2	3	...	12
× 2 table	2	4	6		
× 4 table	4	8	12		
× 8 table	8	16	24		

Use the table to help you calculate:

(a) 12 × 8   **(b)** 15 × 8   **(c)** 23 × 8

2 Ahmed has a collection of racing cars. He puts them in this array.

Write an expression for the total number of racing cars in his collection.

Vocabulary

product: the answer you get when you multiply two or more numbers together.

$$7 \times 8 = \overset{\text{product}}{\boxed{56}}$$

array: items such as objects or numbers arranged in rows and columns.

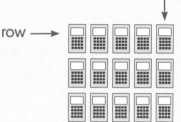

expression: a group of signs and numbers that show how much something is. For example, 5 + 1 is an expression for 6.

Work with a partner to decide how to calculate the answers to questions 3–9. Explain your method and your answer to your partner.

3 Work out the following:

(a) 400 × 9   (b) 60 × 8   (c) 300 × 7

(d) 90 × 6   (e) 700 × 7   (f) 40 × 8

4 What is the product of 700 and 9?

5 Use factors to help you work out the following:

(a) 15 × 6   (b) 18 × 6   (c) 21 × 6

6 This number spider starts with 2 × 3.

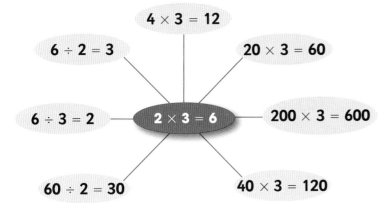

Work with a partner to create your own number spiders.
Start with these multiplication facts:

(a) 4 × 5 = 20   (b) 3 × 6 = 18   (c) 7 × 9 = 63

7 What could the missing numbers be?

(a) **?** × **?** = 150   (b) 160 ÷ **?** = 8

8 What is 5 multiplied by 2 multiplied by 4?

9 Plants are sold in trays of 20.

(a) Florien buys 6 trays of plants.
How many plants is this?

(b) Wayne wants 180 plants.
How many trays must he buy?

Doubling and halving

Let's investigate

SPECIAL OFFER

Buy one cake for $16.

The second cake is half the price of the first cake!

The third cake is half the price of the second cake and so on!

How many cakes can you buy for $31.75?

1   Double the following numbers:

    (a) 36   **(b)** 45   **(c)** 8.3   **(d)** 9.7

2   Halve the following numbers:

    (a) 86   **(b)** 44   **(c)** 14.2   **(d)** 18.8

3   Work out the following:

    (a) double 3.4   **(b)** halve 9.6   **(c)** double 480   **(d)** halve 6600

4   Copy and complete these sequences:

    (a) 70 ──double──▸ 140 ──double──▸ 280 ──double──▸ ?

    (b) 12 ──halve──▸ ? ──halve──▸ ? ──halve──▸ ?

5   Habib is thinking of a number.

Half my number is 8.

What is double Habib's number?

6 This Egyptian papyrus shows the calculation of 13×25 using hieroglyphics.

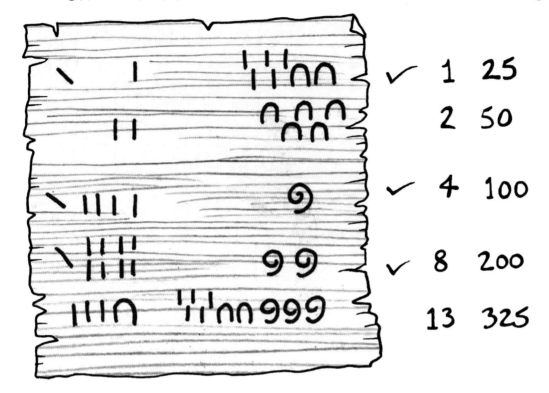

(a) What are the Egyptian hieroglyphs for the hundreds, tens and units?

(b) Can you see how the calculation works? The explaination below shows you; follow the steps from 1 to 4.

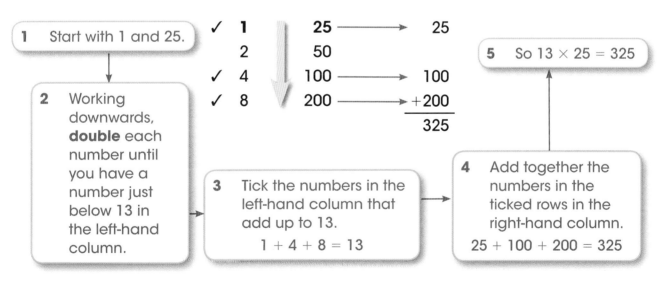

1 Start with 1 and 25.	

2 Working downwards, **double** each number until you have a number just below 13 in the left-hand column.

3 Tick the numbers in the left-hand column that add up to 13.
$1 + 4 + 8 = 13$

✓ 1   25 ⟶ 25
   2   50
✓ 4   100 ⟶ 100
✓ 8   200 ⟶ +200
             325

5 So $13 \times 25 = 325$

4 Add together the numbers in the ticked rows in the right-hand column.
$25 + 100 + 200 = 325$

(c) Use this method to work out these calculations:

(i) 27×78 (ii) 29×56 (iii) 25×48 (iv) 32×76

Subtraction

Let's investigate

Rearrange these digits to make each calculation correct.

Use each digit once for each calculation.

1   2   8   9

$$\boxed{?} . \boxed{?} - \boxed{?} . \boxed{?} = 6.8$$

$$\boxed{?} . \boxed{?} - \boxed{?} . \boxed{?} = 7.4$$

$$\boxed{?} . \boxed{?} - \boxed{?} . \boxed{?} = 0.9$$

Estimate the answer first by rounding the numbers to the nearest whole number.

Vocabulary

difference: the result when you subtract one number from another.

$$\boxed{?} - \boxed{?} = \enclose{circle}{?}$$

difference

1   Sylvester is playing an archery game. He has 9012 points so far. The number he hits with his arrow is subtracted from his score.

(a) After his next go, Sylvester had a score of 2017. Which section of the board did he hit?

(b) Work out all the other possible scores Sylvester could have if he has 9012 points and then shoots one arrow.

(c) Sylvester hit 6008 with his first arrow, then 2996 with his next arrow. What was his score afterwards?

2 The answer to each calculation below is in the yellow box.

Match an answer to each calculation.

(a) 6982 − 3009   (b) 17.1 − 16.8

(c) 4017 − 1995   (d) 8004 − 7987

(e) 8.3 − 3.8   (f) 24.9 − 15.2

(g) 1.3 − 0.9   (h) 1020 − 993

0.3   9.7   0.4

     4.5   3973

27   2022   17

Look at the numbers and think carefully about what method you will use for each subtraction.

3 Class 5 want to encourage wildlife around their school. They have decided to put out bird seed to attract wild birds.

They started with a 12.5 kg bag of black sunflower seeds.

At the end of each week they weighed the bag to find out how much seed had been used.

At the end of week 1 there 9.9 kg of seed in the bag, so 2.6 kg had been used.

Wild Bird Food

Black Sunflower Seeds 12.5 kg

Copy and complete the table.

Week number	Mass of food taken	Mass of the bag at the end of the week
1	2.6 kg	9.9 kg
2	2.1 kg	(a)
3	(b)	5.9 kg
4	2.8 kg	(c)
5	2.7 kg	(d)

Addition

Let's investigate

Each symbol represents one of the numbers 1, 2, 3 or 4.

Match the symbols to the correct numbers to solve the puzzle.

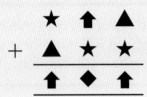

Try one column first and see what the symbols could mean there.

1   This is a page from Adam's mathematics book.

(a)
```
   428
+  337
-------
   755
```

(b)
```
   946
+  544
-------
  1490
```

(c)
```
   535
+  465
-------
  1000
```

(d)
```
   271
+  356
-------
  5127
```

(e)
```
   831
+  848
-------
  1679
```

(f)
```
   689
+  739
-------
  1328
```

To check the answers you could either:
- do the calculation yourself to see if you get the same answer.
- use the inverse operation of subtraction.

Check his calculations to see if they are correct.

If the answer is incorrect, try to find Adam's mistake and write the correct answer.

2 John, Stephanie, Niamh and Daniel are on the TV quiz show 'Number Quest'.

(a) Who has the correct answer?

(b) The prize money is calculated by adding up the scores of the four contestants so far. How much is the prize?

Adding and subtracting money

Let's investigate

Move these purses so that each row and column totals $18.

$9.20 $5.90 $7.10

$2.40 $3.60 $5.20

$1.70 $10.40 $8.50

> Start by making the total of each row $18. Then move the purses within each column.
>
> You could write the amounts on nine pieces of paper and rearrange them on a table.

1. These people are all talking on the phone.

   A: You've spent $26.70. That's fine.

   B: The small one is $10.86 and the big one is $14.58. Our budget is $50, so I think we should get both.

   C: Yes, buy 5. That'll be $24.90.

   D: I spent $9.78 in the café and $13.71 in the shop. I've got $2.51 left.

   E: Yes, that would leave us with $24.56.

   F: I'll buy 3 large at $5.29 and 2 small at $4.75.

   G: I started with $105.30 and I've got $78.60 left.

   H: OK. That will cost $25.37.

   I: I'll buy them on the way home. I have $25 on me – that's exactly enough.

   J: The sale says $5 off when you spend over $25. The shirt is $13.77 and the skirt is $16.23.

   (a) Who is B talking to?   **(b)** Who is I talking to?   **(c)** Who is F talking to?

   (d) Which two people are talking to someone who is **not** listed above?

   (e) Read what the two people from (d) are saying. What might people they are talking to have said?

2 Ruth's family are going to a concert at the theatre for her 11th birthday. Ruth's mum looks on the internet for ticket prices.

	Quantity	Price per ticket	
Standing	1 ▼	$9.27	BOOK
Stalls	1 ▼	$68.45	BOOK
Dress Circle	1 ▼	$45.39	BOOK
Upper circle	1 ▼	$21.58	BOOK

Discounts
For each ticket add a booking fee of $3.86.
Children under 16 get a discount of $4.50 on their ticket price.
Groups over 5 get a discount of $8.94 from the final total.

(a) Ruth's mum wants to book tickets for herself, Ruth and Ruth's little brother in the Dress Circle. How much will that cost?

(b) Ruth's best friend, Amelie, is going to the concert too. She is going with her mum, dad and two little sisters. They are going to sit in the Upper Circle. How much will Amelie's family pay?

(c) Ruth and Amelie saw Luca at the theatre. His grandfather had booked tickets for Luca and his friends for his birthday. Luca and three friends were standing. His grandfather and grandmother were sitting in the stalls. How much did Luca's grandfather pay?

These questions need lots of calculations to answer.
Read the webpage above carefully for all the information.
Make sure you know what the questions are asking for.
You could work with a partner to check that you both do not miss out any calculations.

63

Multiplication and division

Let's investigate

Use the digits 2, 3, 4 and 5 **once** each to make the multiplication that has the greatest product.

? **?** **?** × **?** =

How did you decide where to place each digit?

Discuss how you did it with a partner.

1   184 cubes are arranged in groups of 6.
    How many groups are there?
    How many cubes are left over?

2   There are 8 classes in Year 5 at a school.
    Each class has 29 students in it.
    How many students are in Year 5?

3   Complete three different calculations.

    ? **?** × 3 = 8 **?**
    ? **?** × 3 = 8 **?**
    ? **?** × 3 = 8 **?**

4   Sarah divides $135 equally between 5 children.
    How much does each child receive?

Arrange the digits 1, 1, 1, 2, 3, 5 and 6 to make this calculation correct.

? ? × ? ? = ? ? ?

Find the product of 63 and 58.

193 students are going on a school journey.
They travel by coach and each coach holds 53 students.
How many coaches are needed for the journey?

Handling data

Questions and surveys

Let's investigate

Choose a hypothesis that you would like to investigate.

Write about the information you would need and how you would collect it.

1

> Alpha United and Beta Rovers each played 15 games during one season. Alpha United scored 3 goals in 4 of their matches.

Can you use the information above to answer the question:

'Which is the better soccer team, Alpha United or Beta Rovers?'

Vocabulary

hypothesis: a guess based on knowledge and reason.

data: facts that give you information about something. Data may be given in numbers, words or pictures.

data collection sheet: a prepared sheet you can use for collecting data. For example,

1. Are you male or female?
   ☐ male   ☐ female
2. Are you right-handed or lef-handed?
   ☐ right-handed
   ☐ left-handed

prediction: if you predict something, you say what you think will happen. For example, looking at this sequence of numbers: 4, 7, 11, 13, 16 you can use the pattern to predict that the next two numbers will be 19 and 22.

2 There are four collections of data below: two show the results for Alpha United and two show the results for Beta Rovers.

Match each one to the correct team.

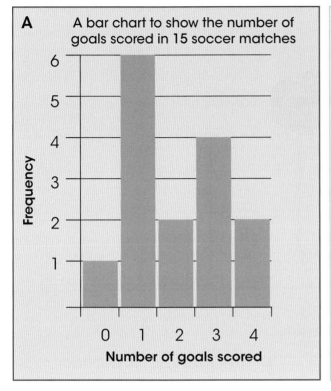

A bar chart to show the number of goals scored in 15 soccer matches

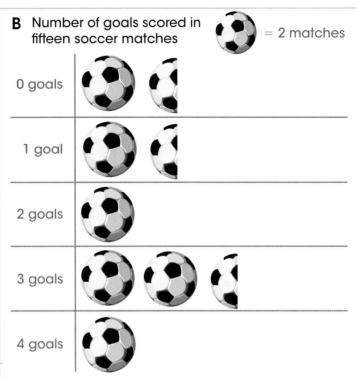

B Number of goals scored in fifteen soccer matches

= 2 matches

C	
Number of goals	**Frequency**
0	1
1	6
2	2
3	4
4	2

D	
Number of goals	**Tally**
0	(((
1	(((
2	((
3	++++
4	((

3 **(a)** What was the highest number of goals scored in a match played by Alpha United?

(b) In how many matches did Beta Rovers score 3 goals?

(c) Which team do you think was the better team?

Discuss with your partner, then write down your answer.

(d) Write down two questions you can answer using the data.

Ask your partner to answer them.

Examining data

Let's investigate
What could be represented by this graph?

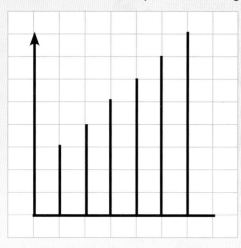

Think about a title, labels for the axes, and questions that could be asked and answered from the data.

Vocabulary

bar line graph: a bar line graph is similar to a bar chart, but lines are used instead of wider bars to show the information.

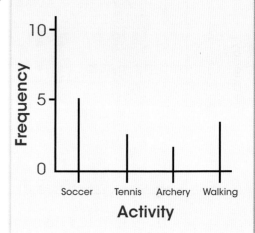

frequency: how often something happens.

frequency table: a table used to record frequency data.

1 Razi collected data about his classmates' favourite animal. He put the data in a table.

Animal	Tally	Frequency
Budgie	‖	
Cat	ⵌ ‖	
Parrot	ⵌ ⵌ ‖	
Fish	ⵌ ‖	
Hamster	‖‖‖	
Lizard	‖	
Rabbit	‖‖‖	
Total		

(a) Copy the table and complete the column showing the frequency.

(b) How many animals did Razi include in the survey?

2 Kirsty bakes cakes to sell at a café.

The pictogram shows the number of cakes she bakes on four days.

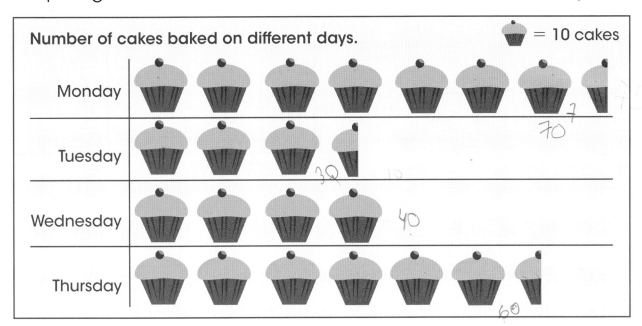

How many cakes did Kirsty bake in total?

3 In a survey, the students at Gateway School chose their favourite fruit drink.

The graph shows the results of the survey.

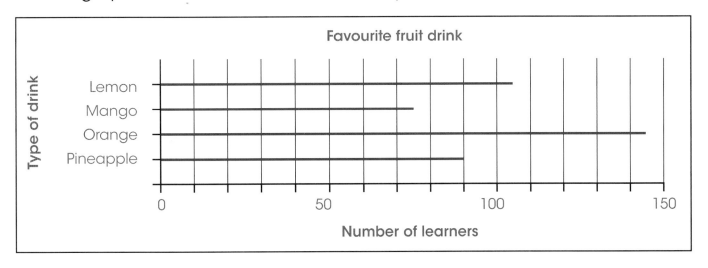

Use the graph to answer these questions:

(a) How many learners chose mango?

(b) How many more learners chose orange drink than pineapple drink?

(c) How many learners took part in the survey?

Turn the page for more questions.

4   This graph shows the
    number of learners
    who chose four
    activities during a
    weekend holiday.

    Number of
    learners

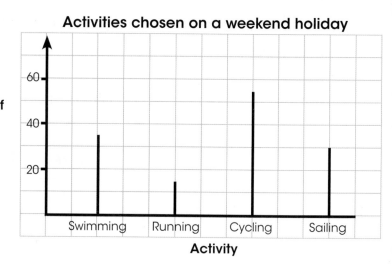

    Use the information
    on the graph to decide
    which of these statements
    are true. Give your answer
    as True or False.

(a) Approximately three times as many learners chose cycling as
    chose swimming.

(b) Cycling was the most popular activity.

(c) All the activities were chosen by more than 20 learners.

(d) The number of learners who chose sailing is approximately double
    the number who chose running.

(e) Approximately 35 learners chose swimming.

5   This graph shows the temperature at midday each day for a week.

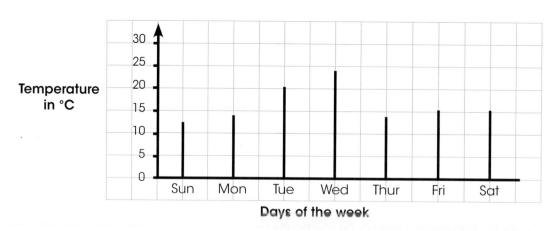

(a) Estimate how much higher the temperature was on Wednesday
    than on Saturday.

(b) Write five questions that could be answered using the information
    on the graph.

    Swap these with a partner, then answer their questions.

6   Three students measured their height and recorded the information in a table.

Learner	Height (cm)
Moira	138
Olivia	121
Parveen	154

The three graphs below show this information.
Which one shows the results best?
Explain your answer.

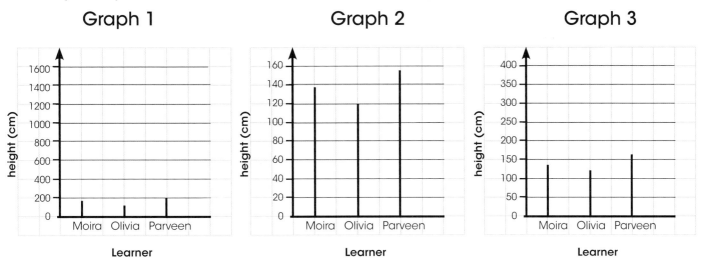

Graph 1   Graph 2   Graph 3

7   Draw a graph to **best** show this information from a survey of shoe sizes.

Shoe size	Frequency
38	5
39	8
40	11
41	18
42	15

Probability

Let's investigate

Here is a spinner in the shape of a regular hexagon.

Make your own spinner that looks like this.

Write 1, 2 or 3 in each section of the spinner so that:

- 1 and 2 are equally likely to be spun.
- 3 is most likely to be spun.

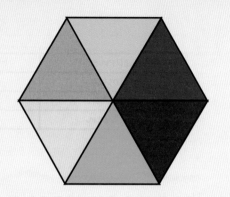

Vocabulary

probability: a measure of how likely it is that something will happen.

likelihood: another word for 'probability'.

fair: something is fair if all results have an equal chance of happening.

 a normal 1–6 dice is fair

 a dice with three sixes is unfair

chance: if something is impossible, it has **no chance** of happening; if it will happen, it is **certain**.

You can use a probability line to show the chances of an event happening.

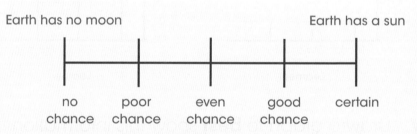

Earth has no moon   Earth has a sun

no chance   poor chance   even chance   good chance   certain

1   Bruno has five T-shirts. He chooses one at random.

Which pattern is he most likely to choose?

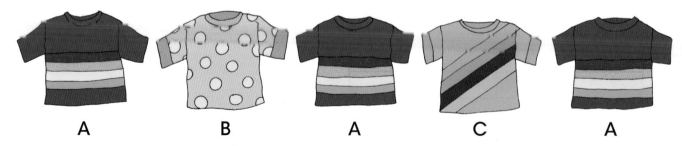

A   B   A   C   A

2 The arrow turns on each spinner.

On which spinner is the arrow most likely to land on a 2?

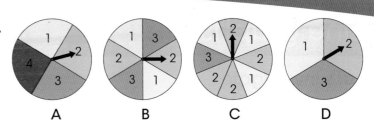

A   B   C   D

3 What is the likelihood of the following events happening? Use the words 'likely' and 'unlikely'.

(a) When you roll a dice you will get a number less than 6.

(b) Someone in your class will lose a shoe this term.

(c) It will rain today.

Make up three statements of your own and say whether they are likely or unlikely.

4 Write an event which has an even chance of happening. How do you know?

5 Lisa has a spinner in the shape of a regular octagon. How likely is she to spin these shapes on the first spin?

Use one of these terms for each answer:
no chance   poor chance   even chance   good chance   certain

(a) a circle   **(b)** a square

(c) an octagon **(d)** a triangle

6 Look at this probability line. Use it to help you answer the following questions.

impossible   unlikely   even   likely   certain

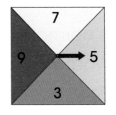

Vincent is using a spinner. What is the likelihood that:

(a) he scores an odd number? **(b)** he scores an even number?

(c) he scores less than 5?   **(d)** he scores a number greater than 6?

7 Petra is rolling a fair dice. What is the probability that:

(a) she rolls a 6?   **(b)** she rolls a 10?

(c) she rolls an even number?   **(d)** she rolls a multiple of 3?

Line graphs

Let's investigate

Write a story which could be represented by this graph.

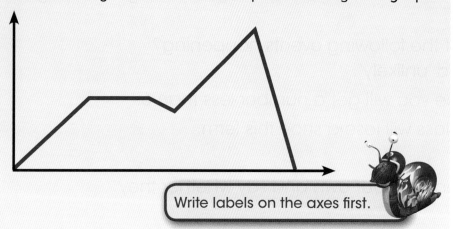

Write labels on the axes first.

Vocabulary

line graph: a graph that uses a line to show how the value of something changes; the line connects plotted points.

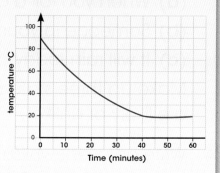

intermediate points: the points between measured values.

1   Fatima was ill during March.
    This graph is her temperature chart.

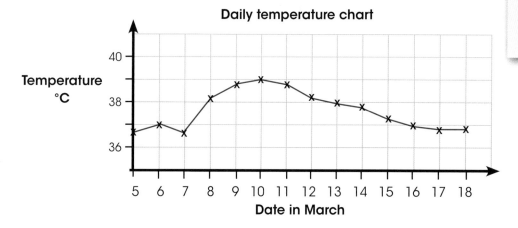

Daily temperature chart

Temperature °C

Date in March

(a) A normal body temperature is 37 °C. What date did Fatima become ill?

(b) What was her highest temperature?

(c) How many days did it take for her temperature to return to normal?
Start counting from when her temperature reached the highest point.

2   Here are the midday temperatures in degrees Celsius in a town during 12 days in January. Draw a line graph to show this information.

Date	1	2	3	4	5	6	7	8	9	10	11	12
Temperature (°C)	2	1	1	4	1	0	−2	−5	−6	−4	−2	0

3 Some learners went on a woodland walk every Tuesday for six weeks.

They collected acorns and pine cones. They counted how many of each they collected and recorded the result on a graph.

Explain why it is not appropriate to join the points together.

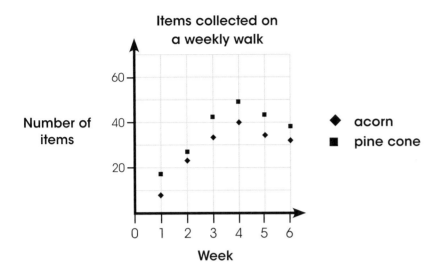

4 This graph shows the temperature in a greenhouse.

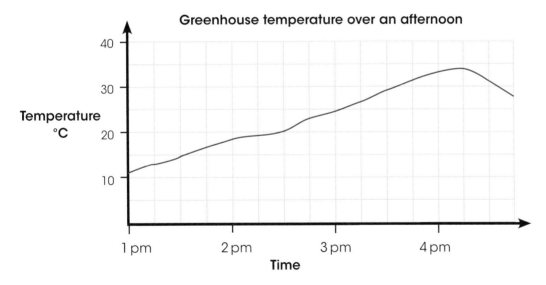

(a) What is each division worth on the vertical axis?

(b) What is each division worth on the horizontal axis?

(c) What was the time when the temperature reached 20 °C?

(d) What was the temperature at 1pm?

(e) Describe what happens to the temperature during the day.

Turn the page for more questions.

5   These graphs show the attendance of Class 5 during one week.
    One of the graphs does not show the data in an appropriate way.

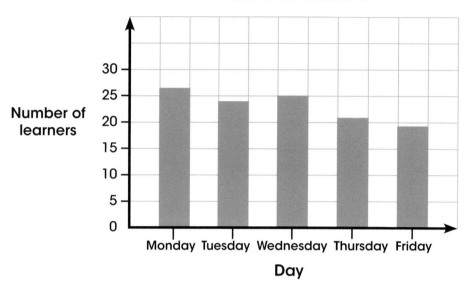

Class 5 attendance

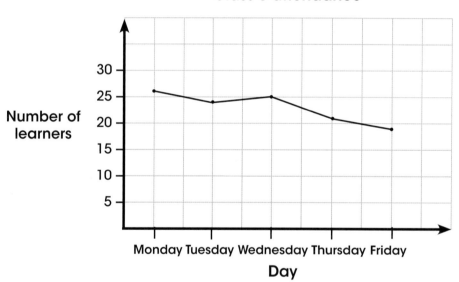

Class 5 attendance

Decide which graph is not appropriate

Discuss your reasons with a partner, then write them down.

6   This graph shows the height of a candle as it burns.

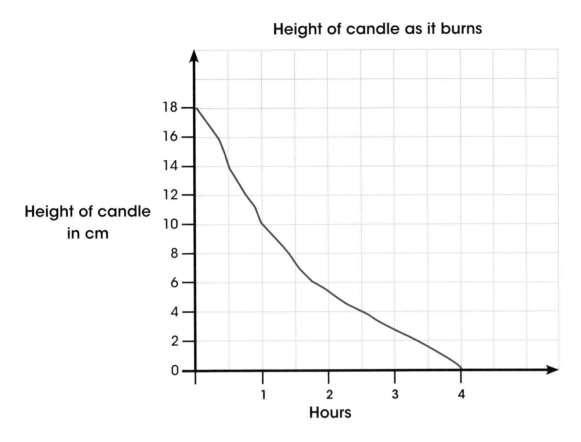

Height of candle as it burns

Height of candle in cm

Hours

(a) How tall was the candle when it was first lit?

(b) How many centimetres of candle burned in the first hour?

(c) What is the height of the candle after 2 hours?

(d) How long does the candle take to burn down from 18 cm to 4 cm?

Finding the mode

Let's investigate

Write a number in each of these boxes so that the mode of the five numbers is 10.

?   ?   ?   ?   ?

> You must make sure that 10 is the most frequent number.

Vocabulary

mode: the data item in a set that occurs most often. For example,

The mode is 1.

There is more than one mode if there is more than one value which appears the most.

For example,

2, **3, 3**, 4, **5, 5**, 7, 8

1 Mariana rolled a dice 10 times and recorded her scores. She did this four times.

What is the mode for each set?

(a) Mode = ?

(b) Mode = ?

(c) Mode = ?

(d) Mode = ?

2 The graph shows the number of children in the families of Year 5 learners.

What is the modal number of children?

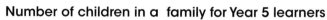

Number of children in a family for Year 5 learners

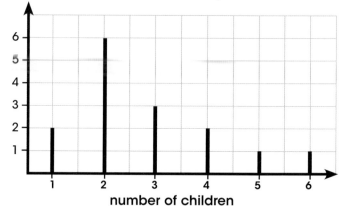

frequency

number of children

3 Find the mode for these data sets:

(a) 2, 5, 3, 2, 4, 10

(b) 2, 3, 0, 10, 4, 5

(c) red, yellow, blue, red, green

(d) elephant, lion, tiger, elephant, monkey

(e) −2, 4, 0, 1, −4

(f) 1, 3, −1, −3, 1, 3

4 Anil asked some learners to name their favourite animal.

The table shows the results of his survey.

What is the mode?

Animal	Frequency
giraffe	4
elephant	10
monkey	4
lion	9
kangaroo	7
panda	8

5 This bar graph shows the number of different cuddly toys sold in a shop last week.

What was the most common cuddly toy sold last week?

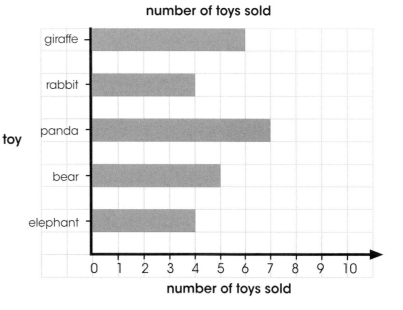

Measure

Measuring and drawing lines

Let's investigate

Angela needed a piece of string at least 5 m long.

She had lots of 50 cm pieces of string. Every time she tied two pieces together she used 50 mm of each piece of string for the knot.

How many pieces of 50 cm long string, does she need to make 5 m?

> You can do the calculation in mm, cm or m. Remember to make sure all the measurements have the same unit.
>
> Imagine three or four pieces of string. Think about what happens when you tie them together. Does this help you understand the problem?

1   Class 5 have been measuring objects in the classroom, but they have made some mistakes.

Some of their measurements are written with the wrong units.

(a) Which items in the classroom have their measurements in the wrong units?

(b) Write the measurements with the correct units for each object.

(c) Choose three objects in your classroom.
Measure one in millimetres, one in centimetres and one in metres.

4   Copy the table below.

Line	Estimate in centimetres	Measurement in millimetres	Measurement in centimetres	Rounded to the nearest centimetre
(a)				
(b)				
(c)				
(d)				
(e)				
(f)				

Estimate the length of each line. Write your estimate in the table.

Measure each line and complete the table.

(a) ————————————————

(b) ————————————————

(c) ████████████████

(d) ——————————

(e) ————————————————

(f) ————————————————

5   Draw straight lines that measure:

(a) 3.2 cm

(b) 89 mm

(c) 67 mm

(d) 10.3 cm

(e) 128 mm

(f) 9.1 cm

Use a sharp pencil.
Check the scale on your ruler.
Find the '0' and the point on the scale you need to make the correct length.

Measuring time

1   Tom takes part in a puzzle game. There are six time puzzles in a set of rooms. Tom can only move into the next room when he has solved the puzzle in the room that he is in.

(a) Tom left the last room at four minutes past ten at night.
The clocks in the rooms show the time when Tom entered each room.
How long did it take Tom to solve each puzzle?

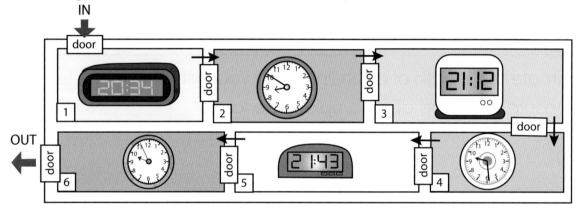

(b) These are the time puzzles Tom solved. Use a clock to time how long you take to solve each puzzle to the nearest minute.

Puzzle 1 This clock is reflected horizontally in a mirror. What is the correct time? 	**Puzzle 2** This clock has been rotated 180° clockwise. What is the correct time? 
Puzzle 3 This clock is 18 minutes slow. What is the correct time? 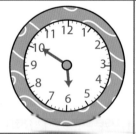	**Puzzle 4** This clock has been reflected vertically in a mirror. What is the correct time? 
Puzzle 5 This clock has been rotated 180° anti-clockwise. What is the correct time? 	**Puzzle 6** This clock is 24 minutes fast. What is the correct time? 

If you had no timer or clock, you could try counting seconds to measure time.

one … two … three …

In spoken English most of the numbers under 100 take less than 1 second to say. Some people use an extra word after each counting number to make the count more accurate. Three words used are 'and', 'elephant' and 'Mississippi'.

one elephant, two elephant, three elephant …

2   Count from 1 to 20 and ask a partner to time you using a stopwatch. Try using 'and', 'elephant' and 'Mississippi' to make the count more accurate.

Which of the words gives you the most accurate count for 20 seconds?

3   Try other words. Can you find a word that makes the count more accurate for you?

4   Sunita and Isobel made a water clock using two empty drinks bottles.

Sunita used a stopwatch to time the drips and Isobel counted the drips. Sunita marked the bottom bottle to show the level of the water after each minute passed. Isobel counted the drips and found that the water had dripped 48 times each time Sunita drew a line.

(a)   Was the water dripping faster or slower than one drip a second?

(b)   At the second line, how much time had passed and how many drips had fallen?

(c)   Approximately how much time has passed on the timer in the picture? How many drips have fallen?

(d)   With a partner, make your own water or sand timer. Make a mark on the timer to show when one minute has passed. Use the timer to time an event in the classroom.

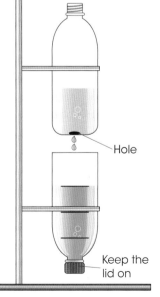

Hole

Keep the lid on

Using calendars

Let's investigate

The first of January is on a Tuesday and the year is not a leap year.

What day of the week is the first of December?

Either work out the day of the week for the first day of each month, or add up all the days of the months between 1st January and 1st December to work out the day.

January

Mon	Tues	Wed	Thurs	Fri	Sat	Sun
	1	2	3	4	5	6
7	8	9	10	11	12	13
14	15	16	17	18	19	20
21	22	23	24	25	26	27
28	29	30	31			

1   Use the calendar to answer these questions.

(a) What day of the week will be the 28th of October?

(b) What are the dates of all the Thursdays in October?

(c) What day of the week will be the first day of November?

(d) What are the dates of all the Fridays in November?

(e) What day of the week will be the 4th of December?

(f) What day of the week will be the last day in December?

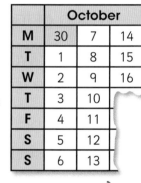

	October		
M	30	7	14
T	1	8	15
W	2	9	16
T	3	10	
F	4	11	
S	5	12	
S	6	13	

2   What is the time interval between these dates?

Give your answer in weeks and days.

(a) 6th October to 28th October

(b) 14th June to 30th June

(c) 31st March to 26th April

(d) 7th January to 7th February

Count on from the start date, **do not** include it in the count.

Example
2nd May to 19th May = 2 weeks and 3 days

84

3 Work out the date of each child's birthday.
Write the day of the week and the date.

4 Tim the Time Traveller uses a special time travelling watch to transport him to to the past or future. He puts in the number of years and months he wishes to travel into the past or future, presses the button, and the watch takes him there.

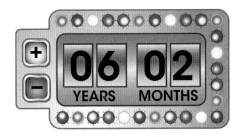

(a) Tim has arrived in April in the year 2028.

Look at the display on the time travelling watch to work out when he came from.

(b) From April 2028, Tim wants to travel to January 2001.

What should he change the watch display to?

(c) From January 2001, Tom changes the watch's display to '– 5 years 4 months'.

What time does this take Tim to?

(d) Tim now wants to get to May 2005.

What should he change the watch display to?

Area (2)

Let's investigate

Class 5 investigated the value of different felt tip pens. They shaded rectangles until the pen ran out.

My 'Penola' pen covered a rectangle 12cm long and 7cm wide.

My 'Top-Tip' pen covered a rectangle 11cm long and 8cm wide.

My 'Fun-Felts covered a rectangle 10cm long and 9cm wide.

Which pen covered the largest area?

Remember that the area of a rectangle can be worked out by multiplying its length by its width.

1   Work out the area of each room on this floor plan.

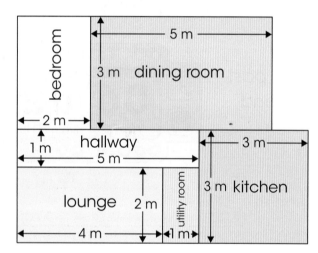

bedroom
5 m
3 m   dining room
2 m
1 m   hallway
5 m
3 m
lounge   2 m
utility room
3 m kitchen
4 m
1 m

2   Measure the length and width of these rectangles to the nearest centimetre and work out the area.

(a)

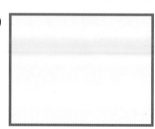

(b)

(c)

3 Mykel used blue and red tiles to make a mosaic pattern.

All of the tiles are 2 cm wide and 3 cm long.

This is a picture of Mykel's pattern.

The tiles are not drawn the correct sizes, so you can't measure it to answer the questions!

(a) What is the area of one tile?

(b) What is the width and length of the whole pattern?

(c) What area of the pattern is blue?

(d) What area of the pattern is red?

(e) What is the area of the whole pattern?

4 For their centenary celebration, Mykel's school asked children to design a new flowerbed.

The total flowerbed had to be a square with an area of 49 m^2.

This is Mykel's design. The red and yellow rectangles are 1 m wide.

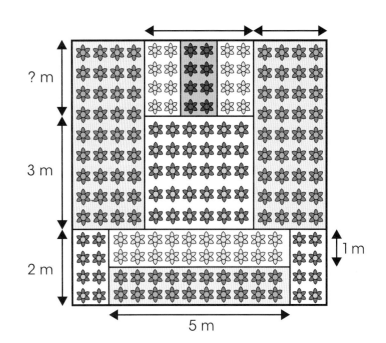

(a) What are the width and length measurements of the whole flowerbed?

(b) What should be the measurement at '? m'?

What is the area covered in:

(c) red flowers?

(d) yellow flowers?

(e) blue flowers?

(f) purple flowers?

(g) Check your answers to questions (c) to (f) by making sure that they add up to the total area of the flowerbed.

Perimeter (2)

Let's investigate

This shape is made from hexagons that each have a perimeter of 30 cm.

What is the perimeter of the whole shape?

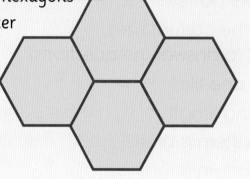

> Work out the length of each side of the hexagons first.
> You could sketch the shape and label the lengths that you know.

1   Use your times tables facts to calculate the perimeter of each of these regular shapes:

    (a) a pentagon with 5 cm sides.

    (b) a hexagon with 9 cm sides.

    (c) a square with 8 cm sides.

    (d) an equilateral triangle with 10 cm sides.

    (e) an octagon with 6 cm sides.

> **Calculating the perimeter of a regular shape**
> To calculate the perimeter of a regular shape, multiply the number of sides by the length of one side.

2   Calculate the perimeter of each rectangle.

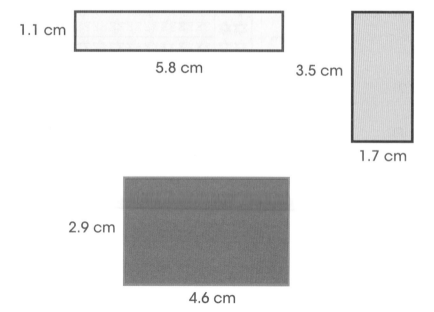

1.1 cm

5.8 cm

3.5 cm

1.7 cm

2.9 cm

4.6 cm

3   Draw three different rectangles that have a perimeter of 22 cm.

4 Look at these triangles.

For each triangle, write down the type of triangle, the length of each side to the nearest millimetre, and the perimeter.

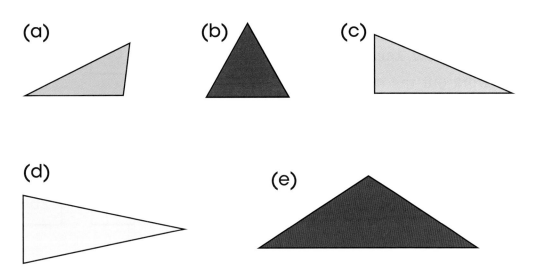

(a)

(b)

(c)

(d)

(e)

5 Investigate the possible length and width of a rectangle that has an area of 20 cm² and a perimeter of 24 cm.
Draw a rectangle with this area and perimeter.

6 Investigate the possible length and width of a rectangle that has an area of 36 cm² and a perimeter of 26 cm.
Draw a rectangle with this area and perimeter.

7 This hexagon is made from equilateral triangles that each have a perimeter of 24 cm.
What is the perimeter of the hexagon?

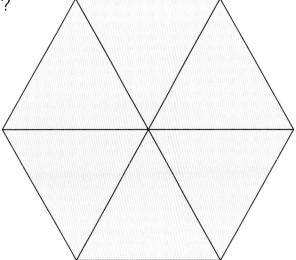

Number

Using mental strategies

Let's investigate

Study the pattern in the first row, then apply it to the other rows to work out the answers.

5	60	12
19		13
17		25

Use your mental skills to help with these investigations.

1 Number chains

Choose any starting number and then apply the following rule:

If the number is even, halve it.

If the number is odd, add 1 and halve it.

Example: $14 \longrightarrow 7 \longrightarrow 4 \longrightarrow 2 \longrightarrow 1$

- Do all chains end at 1?
- Investigate different starting numbers.

2 Persistence of a number

Choose a two-digit number. Multiply the number of tens by the number of units until your answer is a single digit.

Count how many times you multiplied.

This is the **persistence** of the number.

Example: starting with 97

$9 \times 7 = 63 \qquad 6 \times 3 = 18 \qquad 1 \times 8 = 8$

Persistence = 3

- What is the biggest number you can find with persistence 1?
- Can you find numbers with persistence 1, 2, 3, 4 or more?

3 Elevens

$26 \times 11 = 286$

$32 \times 11 = 352$

Multiply other two-digit numbers by 11.

Can you see any patterns?

Discuss your findings with a partner.

Can you find a quick way of multiplying by 11?

4 What's my number?

Work with a partner to find these numbers.

(a) Gabriela says, 'I'm thinking of a number.
I double it and the answer is 38.'

What number is Gabriela thinking of?

(b) Leroy says, 'I'm thinking of a number.
I halve it and the answer is 42.'

What number is Leroy thinking of?

(c) Pierre says, 'I'm thinking of a number.
I double it, then add 4 and my answer is 88.'

What number is Pierre thinking of?

(d) Tara says, 'I'm thinking of a number.
I double it and double it again and the answer is 60.'

What number is Tara thinking of?

5 Ring totals

Copy this diagram and write the numbers 1 to 12 in the circles. Use each number only once.

The total of the numbers in the outside ring must be the same as the total in the inside ring.

Work with a partner.
Discuss ways of solving the problem.

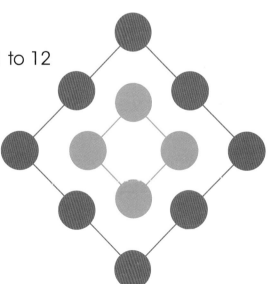

Working with decimals

Let's investigate

Here are three number cards:

Choose two cards to complete the grid below, then find the nearest whole number.

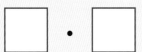

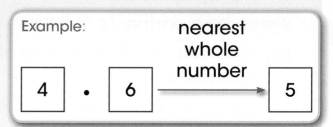

Example:

4 . 6 → nearest whole number → 5

- How many different decimal numbers can you make?
- How many different nearest whole numbers did you find?

1 Here is part of a number line. What number goes in the box?

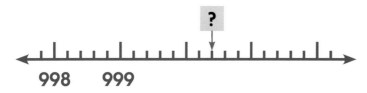

2 Round these numbers to the nearest whole number.

(a) 5.01   (b) 9.52   (c) 6.65

3 The table shows the mass of children when they were born.

(a) Who was the heaviest baby?

(b) Write the masses of the babies in order, starting with the lightest.

Student	Mass (kg)
Bruno	4.35
Carmen	4.78
Daniel	3.81
Ella	5.61
Fatima	4.54

4 What number is exactly half way between six point five and six point six?

5 Write the correct sign < or > between each pair of numbers.

(a) 3.03 **?** 3.8

(b) 4.14 **?** 4.2

(c) 6.78 **?** 6.87

(d) 0.3 **?** 0.13

6 Rearrange these numbers in order of size, starting with the smallest.

(a) 5.05   5.5   5.15   5.51   5.55

(b) 3.13   3.03   3.33   3.31   3.01

(c) 3.13   31.3   3.11   13.1   31.1

7 Which of these numbers is closest in value to 0.1?

0.01   0.5   0.2   0.11   0.9

8 Write these numbers in order, starting with the largest.

4.04   4.24   4.4   4   4.2

9 Ahmed has these cards:

Which numbers can he make between 0 and 40 using all four cards?

10 Here are four digit cards.

Use all four cards to make this calculation correct.

? . **?** + **?** . **?** = 10

Percentages

Let's investigate

Which of these is larger?

> 50% of 100

> 100% of 50

Explain to a partner how you know.

Vocabulary

per cent: the number of parts in a hundred.

percentage (%): the number of parts out of a hundred. $\frac{25}{100}$ squares are shaded. So 25% of the grid is shaded.

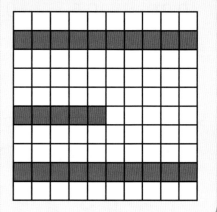

1   What percentage of each diagram is shaded?

(a)
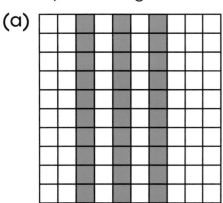

(b)
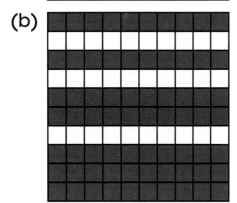

(c)
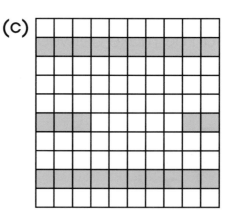

2   Draw diagrams to show the following percentages:

(a) 50%   (b) 75%   (c) 10%   (d) 1%

3   Write these fractions as percentages:

(a) $\frac{13}{100}$ (b) $\frac{23}{100}$ (c) $\frac{78}{100}$ (d) $\frac{1}{10}$ (e) $\frac{7}{10}$

4   55% of a class are boys. What percentage of the class are girls?

5   80% of the learners in Year 5 won an award for good attitude in all lessons.
     There are 100 learners in the year. How many learners won an award?

6   Find 10% of these quantities:

     (a) 40   **(b)** 70 cm   **(c)** $20   **(d)** 120 kg

7   In a sale the marked prices are reduced by 10%.
     How much would be taken off these sale items?

     (a) A book priced at $7.50.

     (b) A jacket priced at $65.

10% off

8   There are 160 passengers on a train.
     25% of the passengers get off at a station.
     How many passengers remain on the train?

9   Copy and complete these percentage diagrams:

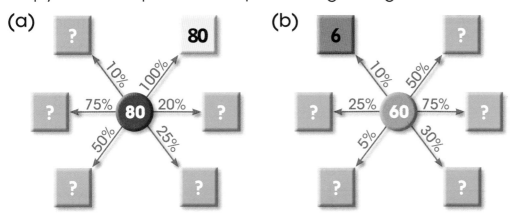

(a)

(b)

10 Bao takes part in a quiz.

     She answers questions on general knowledge and art.

     She gets 60% of the general knowledge questions correct and
     80% of the questions on art correct.

     (a) She answers 10 questions on general knowledge.
          How many does she answer correctly?

     (b) She answers 20 questions on art.
          How many does she answer correctly?

Equivalent fractions, decimals and percentages

Let's investigate

Three pizzas are cut up like this:

 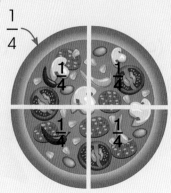 

How can the pieces be shared so that six people have the same amount of pizza?

> Think about how much each person will have.

1   Copy and complete these equivalent fractions.

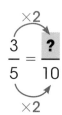 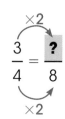 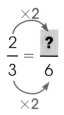

$$\frac{3}{5} = \frac{?}{10}$$ $$\frac{3}{4} = \frac{?}{8}$$ $$\frac{2}{3} = \frac{?}{6}$$

2   Copy and complete this table of equivalent fractions, decimals and percentages.

Fraction	Decimal	Percentage
$\frac{3}{10}$		
		10%
	0.2	
$\frac{23}{100}$		
		25%
	0.7	

Vocabulary

equivalent fractions: are equal in value. For example,

$$\frac{3}{5} = \frac{6}{10}$$

simplest form: a fraction with the numerator and denominator as small as possible. For example,

$\frac{1}{2}$ is the simplest form for the set of fractions $\frac{1}{2} = \frac{2}{4} = \frac{3}{6} = \frac{6}{12}$ etc.

3 This diagram contains an equivalent fraction, decimal and percentage.

Copy and complete these diagrams.

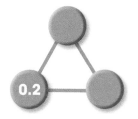

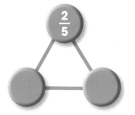

4 Use the numbers in each circle to make fractions and decimals that are equal.

Example: **0 1**
           2 5 $\dfrac{1}{2}$ = **0** . **5**

(a)   **0 5**
      4 8

(b)   **0 6**
      5 3

(c)   **10 0**
       3 3

5 Look at this set of fractions and percentages:

| $\dfrac{75}{100}$ | $\dfrac{3}{10}$ | $\dfrac{10}{100}$ | $\dfrac{15}{150}$ | $\dfrac{50}{200}$ | $\dfrac{1}{10}$ | $\dfrac{1}{2}$ | $\dfrac{25}{100}$ | $\dfrac{3}{4}$ |

| $\dfrac{1}{4}$ | $\dfrac{30}{40}$ | $\dfrac{60}{120}$ | $\dfrac{50}{100}$ | 10% | 75% | 25% | 50% |

(a) Write down four sets of equivalent fractions and percentages.

(b) Copy and complete the table for the fraction you did **not** use.

Fraction	Equivalent fractions		Percentage

6 Look at the groups of fractions, decimals and percentages.
For each group find the odd one out and explain your reasoning.

(a) $\dfrac{5}{10}$, 50%, $\dfrac{3}{6}$, 0.1   (b) $\dfrac{1}{5}$, 20%, $\dfrac{3}{5}$, 0.2

Mixed numbers and improper fractions

Let's investigate

Write down three **different** mixed numbers so that:

- one number is between 1 and 2.
- one number is between 1 and 2 but closer to 2 than 1.
- one number is between 1 and 2, is closer to 2 than 1 and the fraction has a denominator which is an odd number.

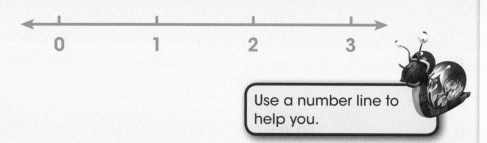

Use a number line to help you.

1 What value do these diagrams show? Write your answer as an improper fraction and an mixed number.

Example:

1	1	1	1
4	4	4	4

1	1	1
4	4	4

$\frac{7}{4} = 1\frac{3}{4}$

(a)

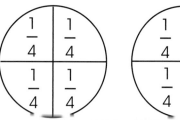

(b)

1	1	1	1	1
5	5	5	5	5

1	1
5	5

1	1	1	1	1
5	5	5	5	5

2   Three pizzas are cut into quarters. How many pieces is this?

3   Change these improper fractions into mixed numbers.

(a) $\dfrac{7}{4}$ (b) $\dfrac{9}{5}$ (c) $\dfrac{10}{3}$ (d) $\dfrac{6}{4}$ (e) $\dfrac{7}{3}$

4   Draw a number line from 0 to 3 and place these mixed numbers on it.

$1\dfrac{1}{4}$ $2\dfrac{3}{4}$ $1\dfrac{7}{8}$

$2\dfrac{1}{2}$ $1\dfrac{3}{8}$ $2\dfrac{1}{8}$

0   1   2   3

Addition and subtraction (2)

Let's investigate

At a school fete, Naomi has to throw four balls
into the buckets and score exactly 600.

How can Naomi score exactly 600?
Can you find more than one way?

1 Work out these calculations:
   (a) 4837 + 1927   (b) 483 + 1978   (c) 7787 + 1498
   (d) 4138 − 2467   (e) 9876 − 7142   (f) 6184 − 982

2 Calculate:
   (a) 28.2 + 13.4   (b) 12.46 + 1.31 (c) 13.41 + 4.39
   (d) 28.2 − 13.8   (e) 123.1 − 47.3 (f) 34.29 − 7.41

3 Solve these problems:
   (a) Find the sum of 48.9 and 34.2
   (b) Find the difference between 78.56 and 65.87
   (c) Fatima has $7.25. She is given $15.50
       How much does she have now?

4 A shop is having a sale and offering
   $2.25 off the cost of these following
   books:
   (a) What is the cost of each book
       in the sale?
   (b) What is the total cost for the
        four books in the sale?

5 Use each of the digits 1, 2, 3, 4, 5, 6, 7, 8 and 9 to complete this addition:

?	?	?	
?	?	?	
?	?	?	+
9	9	9	

6 Use each of the digits 2, 3, 5 and 8 to complete this calculation:

?	.	4	?	
6	.	?	1	+
?	.	9	4	

7 Find the sum of these four numbers: 256, 79, 1089 and 8540.

8 Copy and complete this table.

	Total	Sum	Difference
1147 and 8577			

9 Here are five different numbers.

| 1700 | 2700 | 3700 | 4700 | 5700 |

Use three of these numbers to make this calculation correct.

| ? | + | ? | + | ? | = 13 100 |

10 Use each of the digits 1, 2, 3, 4, 5, 6, 7, 8 and 9 to complete this subtraction calculation:

?	?	?	
?	?	?	−
?	?	?	

Fractions and division

Let's investigate

Each of these numbers gives a remainder of 1 when you divide it by 4:

 5 **13** **41**

We can write the remainder as $\frac{1}{4}$.

For example, $5 \div 4 = 1\frac{1}{4}$

- Find some more numbers that have a remainder of $\frac{1}{4}$ when divided by 4.

- Find some numbers that have a remainder of $\frac{3}{4}$ when divided by 4.

1. A delivery driver loads his van with packages.
   Each package has a mass of 8 kg.
   The maximum mass the van will hold is 804 kg.
   What is the largest number of packages that the van can hold?

2. A company employs 56 staff.
   The company gives each employee three T-shirts as part of their uniform.
   T-shirts are sold in packs of 10. How many packs of T-shirts does the company need?

3. A teacher asks his students to write down the calculation 28 divided by 4.
   Here are five responses. Some are correct and some are incorrect.
   Write down all the correct responses.

$28 \div 4$

$\frac{4}{28}$

$\frac{28}{4}$

$4\overline{)28}$

$4 \div 28$

4. What is the value of each of these?
   (a) one-tenth of 350.   **(b)** one-fifth of 45.   **(c)** one-third of 21.

5. Work out: **(a)** $\frac{1}{4}$ of 24 kg   **(b)** $\frac{1}{8}$ of 32 cm   **(c)** $\frac{1}{3}$ of $15

6 Find: **(a)** $\frac{2}{3}$ of 24   **(b)** $\frac{7}{12}$ of 60   **(c)** $\frac{3}{5}$ of 40

7 Which is the larger amount?

(a) $\frac{2}{3}$ of \$15 or $\frac{1}{2}$ of \$18?

(b) $\frac{3}{4}$ of 36 beads or $\frac{4}{5}$ of 35 beads?

(c) $\frac{7}{10}$ of 40 cm or $\frac{2}{3}$ of 36 cm?

8 Aaron has 20 pictures on a page of his book.

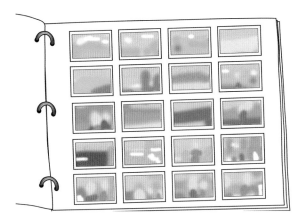

$\frac{1}{4}$ of the pictures show buildings.

$\frac{1}{2}$ of the pictures show animals.

The rest of the pictures show people.
How many pictures are of people?

9 Leroy takes \$40 on a shopping trip. He spends $\frac{1}{5}$ of his money.
How much money does he spend?

10 There are 24 beads on a string.

Three-quarters of the beads are red. Four beads are black.
The rest of the beads are white.

How many beads are white?

11 Sara has a piece of ribbon 5 metres long.

She cuts pieces of ribbon 30 centimetres long.

What is the maximum number of pieces she
can cut from the 5 metre length?

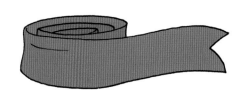

12 Here are five numbers.

$4\frac{6}{10}$ 4.6 $4\frac{3}{10}$ $4\frac{3}{5}$ 4.3

Write down all the numbers from this list that give the **same value** as
dividing 23 by 5.

Using inverse operations and brackets

Let's investigate

Use all the numbers 3, 3, 4 and 8 with any operation signs
and brackets to give an answer of 24.

Now try using these numbers:

1, 2, 2, 7 and then 1, 2, 5, 6

> Think about two numbers
> which multiply together to
> give 24. Try to make these
> using the original numbers.

Vocabulary

brackets: a pair of symbols used to enclose sections of a mathematical
expression. The part in the brackets is calculated first. For example,
$(2 + 7) - 4 = 9 - 4 = 5$.

order of operations: the order in which operations should be done.

1   Match up pairs of calculations that give the same answer.

2×10 $2 \div 10$ $10 - 5$

$10 - 2$ $2 + 10$ 10×2

$2 - 10$ $10 \div 5$ $10 \div 2$

$10 + 2$ $5 \div 10$ $5 + 10$

5×10 $5 - 10$ 10×5

$10 + 5$

2   Calculate:

(a) $(5 + 2) \times 3$ (b) $(3 \times 6) + 4$ (c) $3 \times (8 - 5)$

(d) $(8 - 6) \times 4$ (e) $(3 + 7) \div 10$ (f) $(12 + 6) \div 3$

3 There is a sign missing from each empty box.

Which sign $<$, $>$ or $=$ makes these expressions correct?

(a) $2 \times (3 + 4)$ **?** $(2 \times 3) + 4$ (b) $(10 \times 6) \div 2$ **?** $10 \times (6 \div 2)$

4 Five times a number is 200. What is the number?

5 What are the missing numbers?

(a) $12 \times 5 =$ **?** $+ 37$ (b) **?** $\div 5 = 12$

6 Use $+$, $-$, $\times$ and $\div$ with brackets to make number sentences that give the target number.

Example: $3, 4, 6$ Target 42 Answer $(3 + 4) \times 6$

(a) $2, 5, 6$ Target 40   (b) $3, 5, 6$ Target 21
(c) $3, 4, 6$ Target 12   (d) $2, 7, 10$ Target 6
(e) $4, 6, 10$ Target 1   (f) $3, 6, 15$ Target 3

7 Work out which numbers these learners are thinking of.

Example: Tariq is thinking of a number.
He adds 7 to his number, then divides by 10.
His answer is 1. What number is Tariq thinking of?

Tariq's number is 3

(a) Sonja is thinking of a number. She adds 5 to her number, then divides by 2. Her answer is 6. What number is Sonja thinking of?

(b) Pedro is thinking of a number. He multiplies his number by 3, then subtracts 2. His answer is 4. What number is Pedro thinking of?

(c) Maria is thinking of a number. She divides her number by 3, then adds 11. Her answer is 14. What number is Maria thinking of?

8 Find the missing numbers.

(a) $6 \times$ **?** $= 4.8$ (b) **?** $\times 9 = 0.63$ (c) **?** $\times 90 = 720$
(d) **?** $\div 4 = 6$ (e) $81 \div$ **?** $= 9$ (f) **?** $\div 10 = 3.6$

Ratio and proportion

Let's investigate

Three of these children are describing the same fruit smoothie. Which child is describing a different recipe?

A

$\frac{1}{4}$ of the smoothie is blueberries.

C

For every 1 blueberry, there are 3 raspberries.

B

For every 4 raspberries there is 1 blueberry.

D

$\frac{3}{4}$ of the smoothie is raspberries.

Vocabulary

ratio: used to compare a part against another part.

proportion: used to compare a part against the whole. Fractions can be used to describe a proportion.

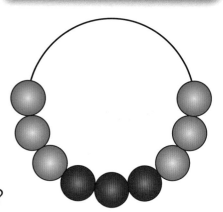

1   Look at the beads on the necklace.

(a) What fraction of the beads are red?

(b) What fraction of the beads are blue?

(c) What is the ratio of red beads to blue beads?

2   You are a jewellery designer.
Draw designs of jewellery that match these descriptions:

(a) a necklace where $\frac{1}{4}$ of the beads are yellow.

(b) a bracelet where for every 5 purple beads there are 2 pink beads.

(c) a pair of earrings where for every 2 green beads there are 3 blue beads.

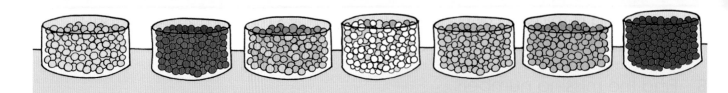

3 One thousand years in the future we take part in the first Solar System football tournament.

Results	
Martians 3 Venusians 2	Saturnians 1 Earthlings 1
Venusians 1 Saturnians 3	Earthings 4 Martians 2
Earthlings 4 Venusians 1	Martians 6 Saturnians 2

Which of the following statements are true, and which are false?

(a) In their match against the Earthlings, the Saturnians scored $\frac{1}{2}$ of the goals.

(b) In the match between the Martians and the Venusians, for every 3 goals scored by the Martians there were 2 goals scored by the Venusians.

(c) In their match against the Earthlings, the Venusians scored $\frac{1}{4}$ of the goals.

4 Tony's dad is a decorator and wants help mixing a new colour. He mixes 1 litre of colour A with 3 litres of colour C to make a new colour called AC.

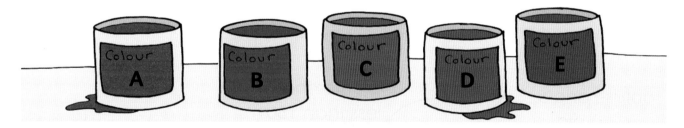

(a) Tony accidentally spills half of his dad's AC mixture. How many litres of A and C does he need to mix together to replace what was spilt?

Tony's dad mixed one and a half tins of B, with 3 tins of D and some of E to get a new colour. He made 8 tins of new colour in total.

(b) How many tins of colour E did he use?

(c) How many tins of each colour would he need to make 16 tins of the new colour?

Geometry

Angles

Let's investigate

Which three of these pieces fit together to make a complete circle?

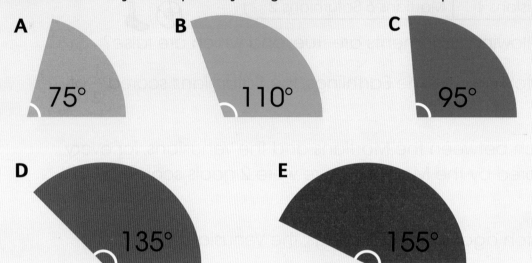

A 75°

B 110°

C 95°

D 135°

E 155°

Vocabulary

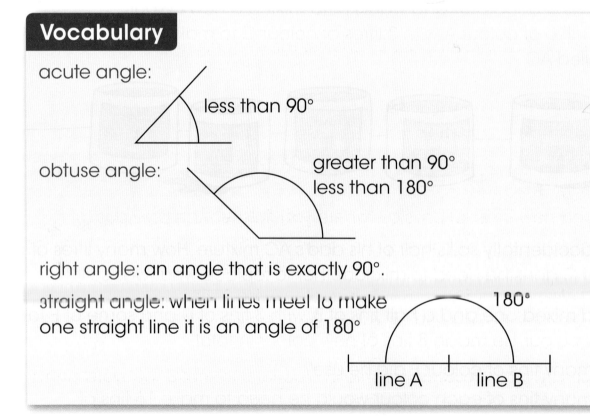

acute angle: less than 90°

obtuse angle: greater than 90° less than 180°

right angle: an angle that is exactly 90°.

straight angle: when lines meet to make one straight line it is an angle of 180°

180°

line A   line B

This is a 360° protractor. You can use the letters placed around the protractor to write secret codes.

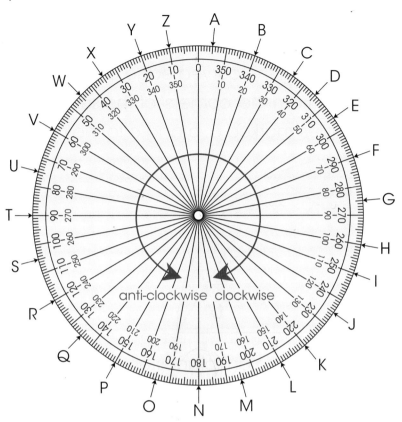

1   Use the 360° protractor decoder to answer these questions.

(a) What letter is at clockwise 150°?

(b) What letter is at anti-clockwise 250°?

(c) What is the angle from 0° to H clockwise?

(d) What is the angle from 0° to H anti-clockwise?

(e) Start at 0°. Follow these instructions.
    For each new instruction, start where you finished the previous turn.
    Write down the letter you stop on after each instruction.
    1 Turn clockwise 35°.   **4** Turn clockwise 155°.
    2 Turn clockwise 75°.   **5** Turn clockwise 115°.
    3 Turn anti-clockwise 230°.   **6** Turn anti-clockwise 95°.
    What word do the six letters make?

(f) Choose a word of your own. Write instructions to make the word using the protractor decoder. Ask a partner to decode your word.

Turn the page for more questions.

2 Investigating angles

Follow these instructions.

1   Use a circular object, or the curved edge of a protractor, to draw a
    semi-circle.

2   Draw a dot anywhere along the curved edge of the semi-circle.

3   Use a ruler to draw lines from the 'corners' of the semi-circle to the dot.

4   Measure the three angles marked a, b and c to the nearest 5°.

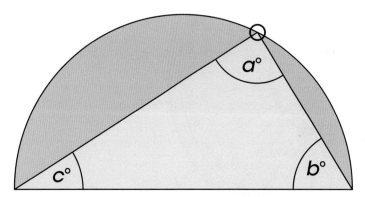

Repeat by marking the dot in different places on the curved edge
of the semi-circle.

Copy and complete this table for the three measurement made
for five different dots.

	Angle at *a*	Angle at *b*	Angle at *c*
dot 1			
dot 2			
dot 3			
dot 4			
dot 5			

Write a sentence to describe any patterns you have found in the angles.

Share any patterns you find with a partner.

3

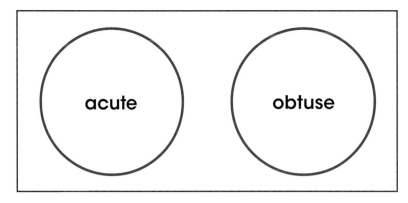

35°	80°	110°
	170°	20°
150°	65°	125°

(a) Make a copy of the Venn diagram.
Sort the angles in the green box into 'acute' and 'obtuse.

(b) Choose two of the acute angles and two of the obtuse angles.
Without using a protractor, draw your best estimate for each angle.
Label the angles with your estimate.
Use a protractor to check the size of the angles you have drawn.

4 Jaret makes a plan to show the angle of the spotlights for the school play.
Work out (do not measure) the missing angles a, b, c and d.

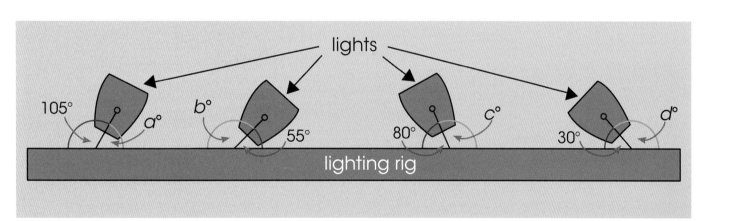

Triangles (2)

Let's investigate

Choose one of these triangles as the 'odd one out'.

Explain how it is different from the others.

Use mathematical vocabulary.

1   Finish each of these sentences to describe the properties of each triangle.

    (a) An equilateral triangle is … /   **(b)** An isosceles triangle is … /

    (c) A right-angled triangle is … /   **(d)** A scalene triangle is … /

2   Write 'true' or 'false' for each of these statements.

    If the statement is true, draw a triangle to match the statement.

(a) An equilateral triangle can be an acute triangle.

(b) An isosceles triangle can be an acute triangle.

(c) An equilateral triangle can be an obtuse triangle.

(d) An isosceles triangle can be an obtuse triangle.

(e) An equilateral triangle can be a right-angled triangle.

(f) An isosceles triangle can be a right-angled triangle.

3   Marianne needs two more pieces of glass to finish her stained
    glass window.

    One piece needs to:

    • have lengths of sides that are 4.3 cm, 5 cm and 2.4 cm.

    • have angles that are 95°, 60° and 25° (to the nearest 5°).

    The other piece needs to:

    • have lengths of sides that are 3.6 cm, 3.2 cm, 1.6 cm.

    • angles that are 90°, 65° and 25° (to the nearest 5°).

    Use a ruler and a protractor to find the two pieces of glass than Marianne
    needs to complete her window.

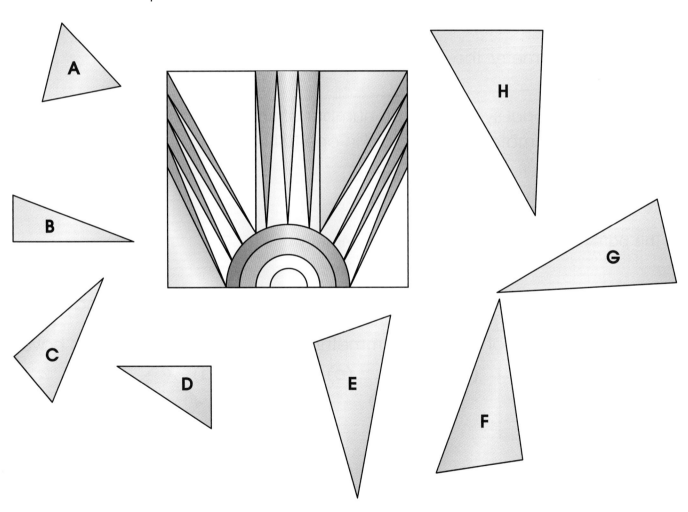

Symmetry in polygons

Let's investigate

This is the Jamaican flag.

What kind of symmetry does it have?

Think about your favourite flag.
What is the order of its rotational symmetry?
How many lines of reflective symmetry
does it have?

You could trace the shapes using tracing paper, and then rotate them on top of the original shapes.
You could fold the tracing paper to find the lines of reflective symmetry.

Vocabulary

rotational symmetry: the outline of a turning shape matches its original shape.

order of rotational symmetry: the number of times the outline of a turning shape matches its original in one full rotation.

This pattern has an order of rotational symmetry of 3.

1 What order of rotational symmetry does each of these shapes have?

2 How many lines of reflective symmetry does each of these shapes have?

(a)   (b)   (c)   (d)

(e)   (f)   (g)

Symmetry in patterns

Let's investigate

This tile pattern is going to be reflected in these mirror lines.
What will be the colour of the square marked 'X'?

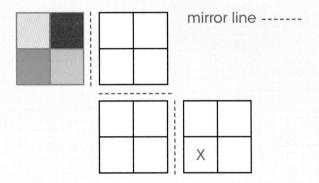

1   If the tile pattern below is reflected in the two mirror lines, what
    colour will these squares be?

(a) A   (b) B   (c) C   (d) D
(e) E   (f) F   (g) G

On squared paper recreate this pattern and colour the rest of
the pattern as it would be reflected in the two mirror lines.

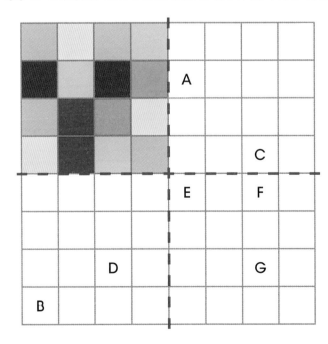

3D Shapes and nets

Let's investigate

Lee has a triangular prism made from modelling clay.

He cuts it straight through with a sharp knife and looks at the faces of the two new shapes he has made.

Which of these shapes could **not** be one of the faces of the new shapes?

triangle   rectangle   trapezium   rhombus

Vocabulary

prism: a 3D shape with two identical parallel faces. All other faces are rectangles. For example,

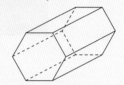

hexagonal prism

pyramid: a 3D shape with a polygon face and triangular faces that meet at a point. For example,

pentagon-based pyramid

1 Write down the 3D shape each net would make.

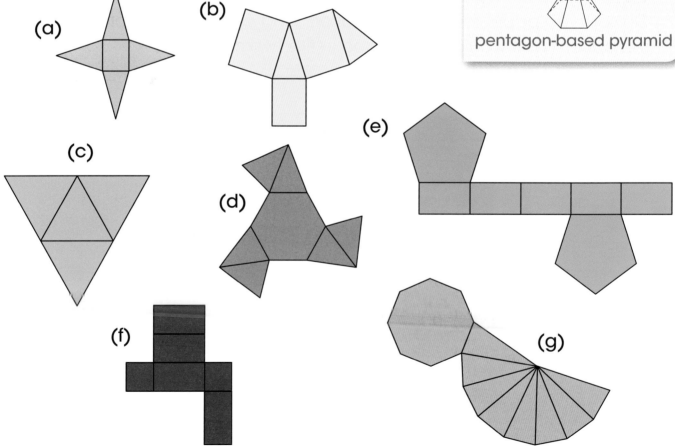

(a)

(b)

(c)

(d)

(e)

(f)

(g)

2   Which of these nets would fold up into a prism?

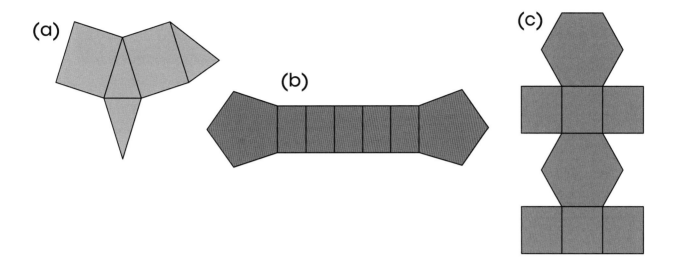

(a)

(b)

(c)

3   Write a set of instructions to help someone decide if a net will fold
    up to make a prism.

4   Which of these nets can fold up into a pyramid?

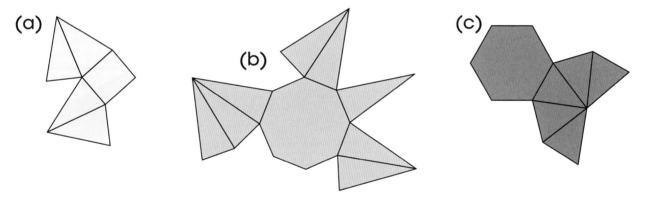

(a)

(b)

(c)

5   Write a set of instructions, to help someone decide if a net will fold
    up to make a pyramid.

Co-ordinates and transformations

Let's investigate

Plot (2, 1) and (4, 3) on a grid.

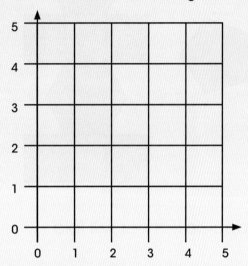

Vocabulary

transformation: changing the position or size of an object by reflection, translation, rotation or enlargement.

Find two more points on the grid that make a square with the two plotted points.

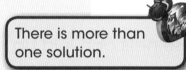

There is more than one solution.

1. For each of these questions, try to visualise where the reflection would be first. Then use a mirror or tracing paper to check.

   What are the co-ordinates of the:

   (a) isosceles triangle when it is reflected in the mirror line?

   (b) square when it is reflected in the mirror line?

   (c) hexagon when it is reflected in the mirror line?

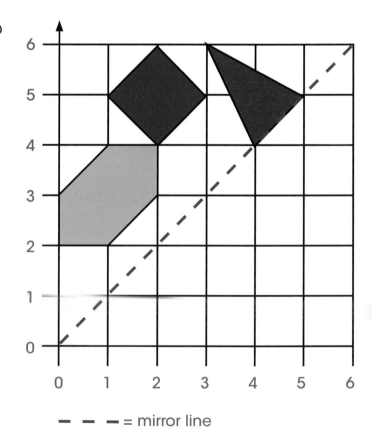

− − − − = mirror line

2 Use translation to move the hexagon through the maze to the EXIT. Write a set of instructions.

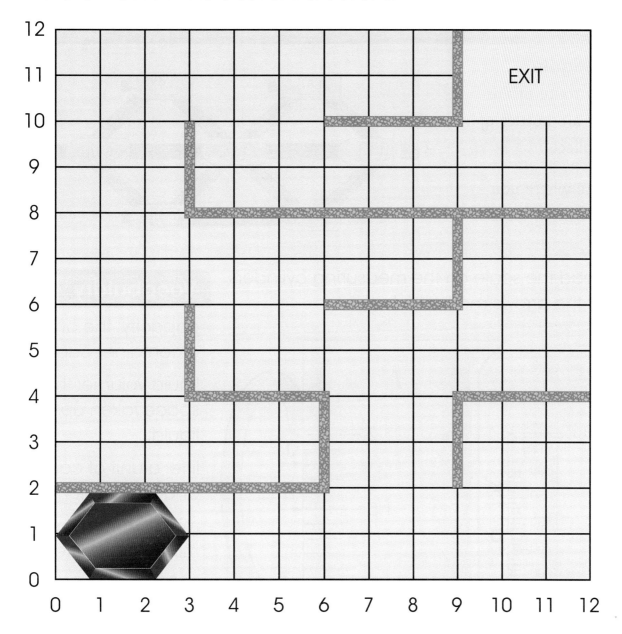

3 Work with a partner.

(a) Place a counter on part of the maze grid above. Challenge your partner to give translation instructions to move the hexagon through the maze to the counter.

(b) Ask your partner to place a counter in the maze. Now it is your turn to give translation instructions to move the hexagon through the maze to the counter.

Measure

Volume, capacity and mass

Let's investigate

Along each route of this maze there are bottles of water to collect.

Find a route where you collect 3600 ml of water.

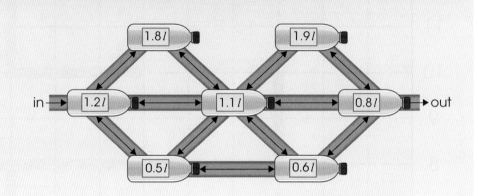

in → 1.2*l* ← 1.1*l* ← 0.8*l* → out

1.8*l*   1.9*l*

0.5*l* ← 0.6*l*

1. **(a)** Read the scale on the measuring cylinders at the arrows marked A to K.

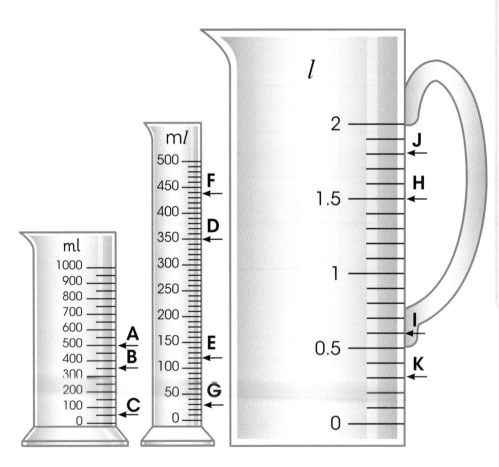

Vocabulary

capacity: the amount a container can hold.

liquid volume: the space taken up by a liquid.

litre: a unit of capacity and liquid volume.

millilitre: there are 1000 millilitres in a litre.

1000 ml = 1l

(b) Convert the measurements on the litre measuring jug into millilitres.

2 Round each of these measurements in litres to the nearest litre.
   (a) 6.1 litres   (b) 9.9 litres   (c) 8.2 litres
   (d) 0.7 litres   (e) 11.5 litres   (f) 5.4 litres

3 This is Francesca's recipe for vegetable casserole. It serves 4 people.

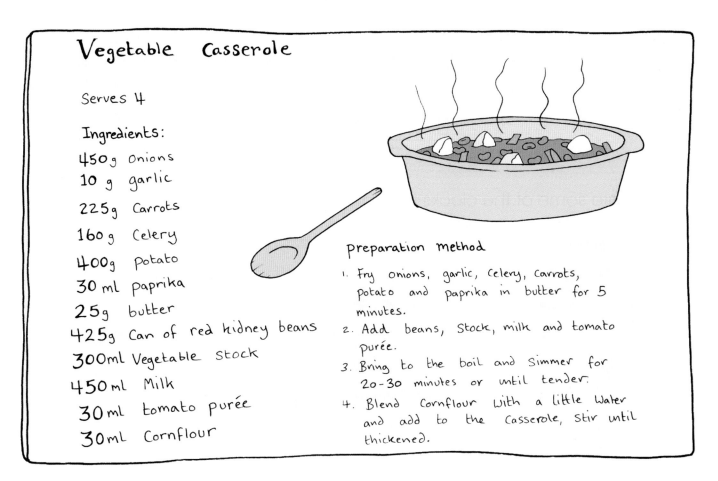

Vegetable Casserole

Serves 4

Ingredients:
450g Onions
10 g garlic
225g Carrots
160 g Celery
400g potato
30 ml paprika
25g butter
425g Can of red kidney beans
300ml Vegetable stock
450 ml Milk
30 ml tomato purée
30ml Cornflour

Preparation method

1. Fry onions, garlic, celery, carrots, potato and paprika in butter for 5 minutes.
2. Add beans, stock, milk and tomato purée.
3. Bring to the boil and simmer for 20-30 minutes or until tender.
4. Blend Cornflour with a little water and add to the casserole, stir until thickened.

(a) If Francesca wanted to make vegetable casserole for 8 people, how much butter would she need?

(b) If she made the recipe for 2 people, how much milk would she need?

(c) If she made the meal just for herself, how much celery would she need?

(d) Francesca is hosting a party for 32 people.
    Write out the list of ingredients with the amounts needed for 32 people.

4 × 8 = 32

(e) Explain how you increased the amounts needed from 4 people to 32 people.

More about time

Let's investigate

Move two matches to make the time 'half past four', as would be seen using digital digits.

Do not overlap the matches.

The answer is in 12-hour digital clock notation.

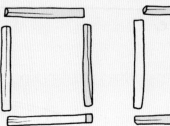

1   Here are some of the clocks in a town clock museum.

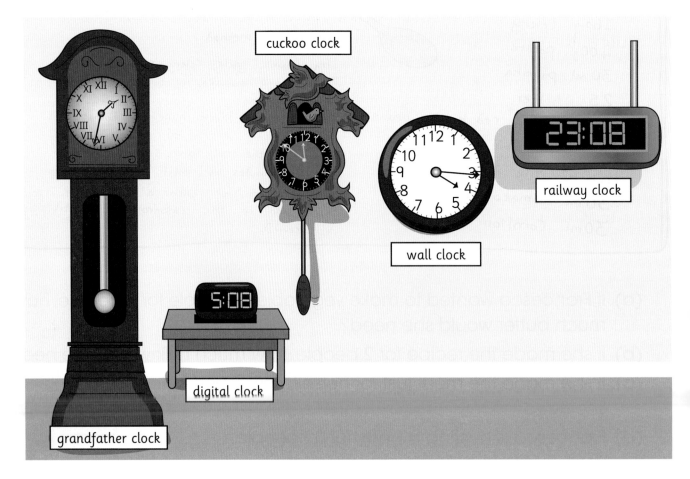

cuckoo clock

railway clock

wall clock

digital clock

grandfather clock

(a) Write the times shown on each clock in words.

(b) If the cuckoo clock and the grandfather clock are both showing 'am' times, what is the difference between the times on the two clocks?

(c) If the grandfather clock is showing an 'am' time and the cuckoo clock is showing a 'pm' time, what is the time interval between the times on the two clocks?

(d) None of the clocks are more than 3 hours ahead of the correct time. None of the clocks are more than 3 hours behind the correct time. What is the correct time in the museum?

2 Mateo noticed that the bath tap in his house was leaking.

He wondered how much water was being wasted each day.

He put a container under the tap to catch the drips. He did this at 10 am. Mateo poured the collected water into a measuring container six times during the day.

The picture below shows the volume of water in the measuring container at each of the six times Mateo added more water.

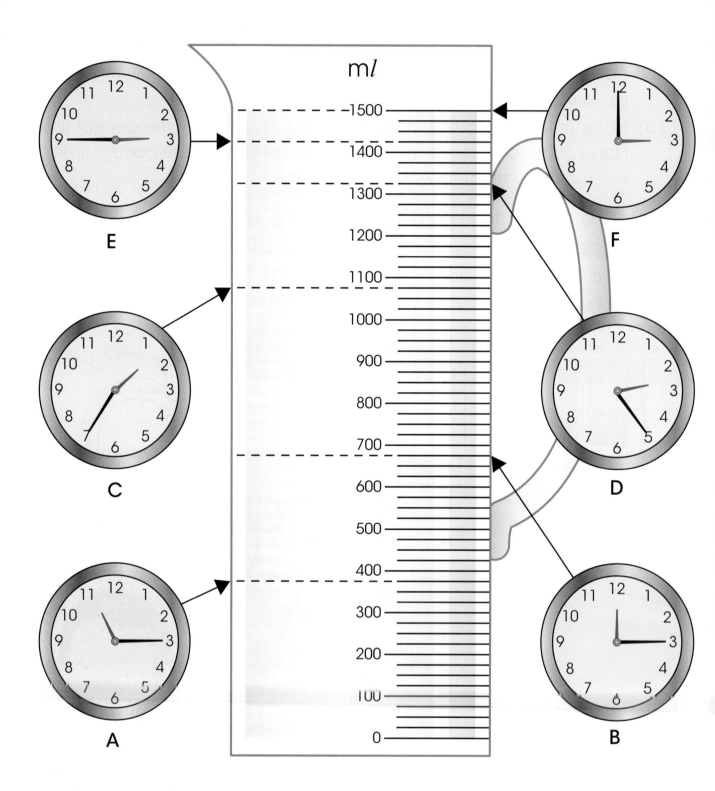

(a) Copy the axes below carefully on to graph paper. Plot points on the grid to show the amount of water Mateo collected.

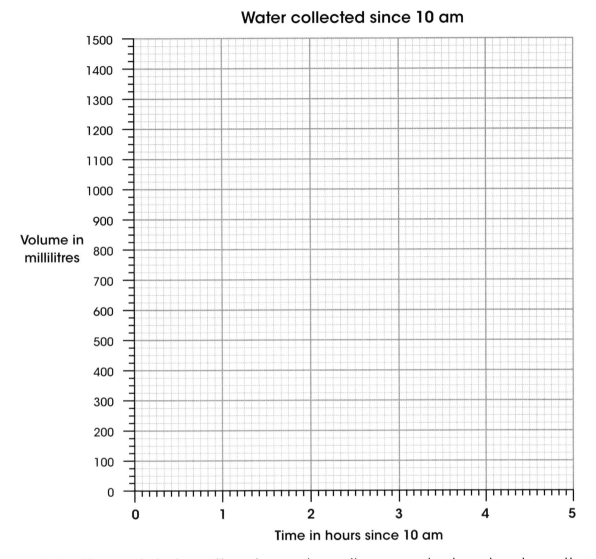

Water collected since 10 am

Volume in millilitres

Time in hours since 10 am

Join the points together to make a line graph showing how the amount of water increased during the day.

(b) Use your graph to find out how much water had been collected at 13.00.

(c) At what time had 550ml of water been collected?

(d) How long did it take for Mateo to collect 1 litre of water? What time was that?

(e) Using what you know about ratio, work out how much water Mateo would have collected if he continued until one o'clock the next morning.

Area and perimeter

Let's investigate

Find a rectangle that has a perimeter double the rectangle's area in square centimetres.

?

> Try different rectangles to find one with a length in centremetres that matches the statement. Remember that a square is also a rectangle.

1   Celia has been rolling pastry. She measures the rectangle of pastry and it is approximately 20 cm wide and 30 cm long.

   20cm

   30cm

(a) What is the area of Celia's pastry?

(b) Celia rolls the pastry across its width. The length stays the same, but the width increases by 8 cm. What is the area of the pastry now?

(c) Finally, Celia rolls the pastry across its length. This time the width stays the same but the length increases by 6 cm. What is the new area of the pastry?

2 Celia is going to make pies in each of these pie dishes. The top edges of the pies will be decorated with shapes made from pastry.

(a) Work out the perimeter of each pie dish so that Celia can plan her decoration.

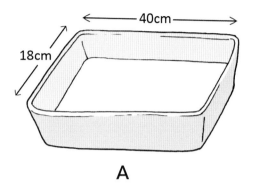

A

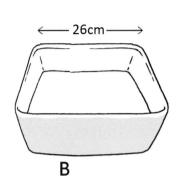

B

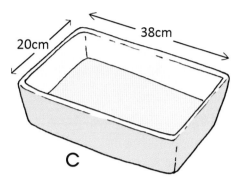

C

(b) Which pie dish needs the greatest area of pastry to cover the top?

3 Measure the perimeter of each of these shapes to the nearest millimetre.

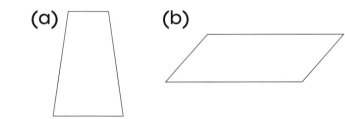

(a) (b)

> Think about what you know about the properties of 2D shapes and recognising symmetry.
> If two sides of the shape are the same length, you only need to measure one of them.

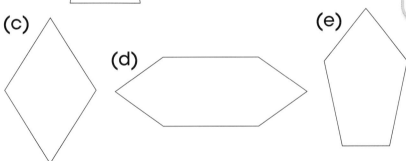

(c) (d) (e)

4 Celia decorates the tops of the pies with the pastry shapes and draws a line of icing around the decoration.

The pink link on these patterns shows how she ices the decorations. Use the measurements of the pastry pieces to calculate the length of the pink icing line on each decoration.

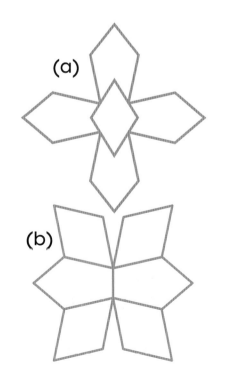

(a)

(b)